THE SHIH TZU

Ch. Greenmoss Chin-Ki of Meo

Ch. Ta Chi of Taishan

THE SHIH TZU

AUDREY DADDS

Foreword by C. R. Duke

Sixth Printing—1983

HOWELL BOOK HOUSE Inc.
230 Park Avenue
NEW YORK, N.Y. 10169

POPULAR DOGS PUBLISHING CO LTD
3 Fitzroy Square, London W1

An imprint of the Hutchinson Publishing Group

Published 1975 by Howell Book House Inc.
230 Park Avenue
New York, New York 10169

First published 1974
© Audrey Dadds 1974

Library of Congress Catalog Card No. 75–13607
ISBN 0-87605-309-6
Printed in U.S.A.

I dedicate this book to

Mona, Lady Brownrigg

who pioneered this breed with so much care, always emphasising the importance of retaining its wonderful character while breeding to perfect its body.

CONTENTS

ILLUSTRATIONS

Foreword by C. R. Duke

There is no doubt that an authoritative and comprehensive book on the Shih Tzu has been needed for a considerable time. Over the last few years we have seen a tremendous rise in popularity of the breed, not only in England and on the Continent, but also in the United States.

Many are the side effects of sudden popularity. Increased classification at shows has created a shortage of experienced judges, which in turn has resulted in too much importance being given to coat, colour and glamour, to the detriment of conformation, type and soundness. Another adverse trend is the indiscriminate breeding by inexperienced people for financial reward.

I hope that this book by Audrey Dadds, Championship Show Judge, member of the committees of the Shih Tzu Club and the Manchu Society, Shih Tzu breeder of long standing, exhibitor and owner of champions, will remind each one of us of our responsibilities towards the breed. Remember that we have been entrusted with the future well-being of our beloved Shih Tzus!

Author's Introduction

I greatly appreciate the honour of being asked to write about the Shih Tzu, which has been no simple task. Much of my knowledge of the breed was learned direct from the late Lady Brownrigg, whose meticulously kept records and old letters have supplied a large part of the early English history. Even so, without the help and encouragement I have received from my husband and Charles Duke throughout the writing of the book, I doubt whether it would have been completed.

My very grateful thanks are also due to the following: Mr. Alan Roger, for passing on his knowledge of the breed in the East, and for his informative pictures and advice and help on early history; Mrs. Audrey Fowler for her early knowledge of the breed; my daughter Alison for her painstaking photography; the late Mr. R. H. Clover, M.R.C.V.S., for kindly checking the accuracy of chapter 12. The help and co-operation I received from Mrs. Gay Widdrington and other breeders are greatly appreciated, and I am only sorry that it was not possible to include all the photographs they were good enough to send.

I am also particularly indebted to Mr. Harry Glover for the excellent line drawings which he has kindly contributed, and to Mrs. Gwen Teele, of Australia, and the Shih Tzu Club of America for overseas information.

A.L.D.

I

Early History – Chinese and Tibetan

Tibetan background

THE origin of the Shih Tzu is somewhat obscure. It is classified as a Chinese dog, since it was bred there for many hundreds of years, but is considered to have originated in Tibet where it was kept in the temples and occasionally given to the Emperors of China as a tribute gift.

According to Snellgrove and Richardson's *A Cultural History of Tibet*, records suggest that Tibet was a barbaric country inhabited by nomadic tribes of Eastern Asian descent. Myth and superstition abounded; the founder of the Yarlung dynasty was said to have come from heaven on a 'sky-cord', leaving no mortal remains on earth. He preceded the great King Srong-brtsan-sgam-po (A.D. 627–50), who established his palace at Lhasa in A.D. 639 and from whose time written historical records began.

The *T'ang Annals* give an account of the relationship between China and Tibet from the seventh to ninth centuries, during which period the two countries were in close contact. From the seventh century onwards, Tibet entered upon a new period of growth and development. On one occasion Tibetans captured the Chinese capital Ch'ang-an-(Sian), and were considered a formidable threat even from the viewpoint of learning. Following a request from a Tibetan envoy for copies of the Chinese classics, a Chinese minister commented 'They have a warlike nature, yet are steadfast in purpose, intelligent and industrious, intent on learning undistractedly.'

King Srong-brtsan-sgam-po was a force to be reckoned with, and in A.D. 640 he and one of his heirs were given Chinese princesses as brides. Occasional marriages may also have taken place between Tibetan nobles and Chinese brides, since the granting of princesses to neighbouring 'barbarian' rulers formed part of Chinese diplomacy.

B

This is not intended to be a historical account of Tibet, but a small part of the early history does illustrate the close association between the two countries and the consequent possibility of an interchange of dogs.

There are records of dogs in Tibet from early times, for example Tibetan mastiffs who guarded the towns and caravans, and also small house dogs which had good hearing and were used to alert the ferocious mastiffs. Both types had thick shaggy coats.

Myth and superstition

Buddhism and the mythological lion play a large part in the development of the lion dogs. Introduced from India, Buddhism took the form of Lamaism, and eventually spread throughout Tibet; this form was not adopted in China until the time of Kublai Khan in 1253.

In Tibet dogs are sacred animals, and the people believe that the souls of erring priests enter into them. The small lion dogs are kept for temple duties and as house pets, where they live as members of the family. The great worship of the lion which forms part of Buddhism, and is particularly prominent in its more mythical form of Lamaism, is considered to be bound up with other, earlier religions. The Buddha Manjusri, the god of learning, is said to travel the four continents as a simple priest, accompanied by a small 'ha pah' (pet) dog. In an instant the dog can be transformed into a mighty lion with Buddha riding on its back.

There are true or 'spirit lions' and 'dog lions'. Images of the spirit lions occur in sacred places such as carvings on the pillars of temples, while the dog lions are the earthly beasts known as the menagerie. The Lamas teach that the true lion is a mountain spirit, which possesses the power of instantaneous projection through space, can become visible or invisible at will, and is similarly capable of infinite expansion or reduction in size. According to the Samye-Ling Tibetan centre which was established in Scotland in April 1967, 'The Shih Tzu, which is a house pet in Tibet, as is the Apso, has a very strong resemblance to a symbolic creature, the Gang Sing or Snow lion, and is part of Ancient Imagery in which he is considered the King of Animals, and is so powerful that when he roars seven dragons fall out of the sky. The three powers which he has are, the ability to leap, then turn in an instant and come back, to walk in mist and clouds, and his voice, the voice of the Middle Way (of truth and fearlessness) subdues all.' (*Manchu News Letter.*)

This could well be a description of the present-day Shih Tzu. It can be assumed that the Tibetan Lamas encouraged the tendency to breed these dogs to resemble their 'lions', and undoubtedly their best specimens would have been selected to be taken as tribute gifts to China.

The lions were not indigenous to China but from A.D. 87 were imported as gifts to the Emperors. Few artists had access to these beasts, and therefore modelled their lions on their own conceptions allied to the use of Buddhist and Lamaist representations. The Lamaist lion is depicted with a harness, to exemplify the subjection of the fiercest passions to the gentle influence of Buddhism, and also has an orb or cub under its foot which have their own symbolic meaning. The earlier Chinese lions have neither harness, ball nor cub.

Tribute gifts

To be given a lion dog was a great honour, and the last tribute gift to the Chinese Emperors was made in 1908, when the Dalai Lama visited the Empress Dowager some months before her death, bringing several dogs. According to Collier in *Dogs of China and Japan in Nature and Art*, these were seen by several foreigners who described them as being similar to the breed of lion dogs then existing in Peking, and known by authentic testimony to have existed there for at least forty years previously. The journey from Lhasa to Peking would take eight to ten months by caravan.

Earlier gifts to Manchus

In 1644 Peking was captured by the Manchus, who had already embraced the Lamaist form of Buddhism. They conquered Tibet in 1645, and the Dalai Lama visited the Emperor of China in Peking in 1653. It was considered that the popularity of the 'lion-like' dogs at the court of the Manchu Emperors was due not only to their affection for animal curiosities but also because of the association with Buddha and his pet dog. The Emperors, being regarded as the personification of the Sun and Sons of Heaven, were seen by the flatterers who surrounded them as symbols of Buddha. This comparison was encouraged by the Tibetan Lamas, and Chinese authorities maintain that they originated the dynastic name of Manchu, basing it on the Tibetan name Manjusri for Wen Shu (the Chinese Buddha), and hence calling the rulers the Man Chu Hsi Li Emperors.

The Emperors were continually followed by their small pet dogs, who heralded their entrance by barking; this was the signal for all servants to avert their faces.

It is believed that the custom of sending these 'shock' dogs from Tibet originated in the early period of the Manchu Dynasty.

Early Chinese dogs

There are certain authenticated facts making it possible to follow to some extent the breeding of dogs in China which could possibly be the ancestors of our Shih Tzu.

From the time of Confucius, around 500 B.C., there are records of 'small' and 'short faced' dogs in China. In the British Museum, there is a skull of an early short-nosed dog which has the bones of the nose natural and unbroken; this seems to disprove the assertion that the Chinese broke the nose bones of young puppies with a chopstick to make them short.

There are clear records of small dogs being imported from Turkey, Persia and Russia, and one of the most interesting is given by both Collier in *Dogs of China and Japan* and Lauffer in *Chinese Pottery of the Han Dynasty*. It seems that in A.D. 624 a pair of small dogs were imported from Fu Lin in Turkey, and right up to the 17th century their descendants were referred to by the Chinese literati as dogs of Fu Lin. Their measurements are given as 6 (Chinese) inches high by 1 (Chinese) foot long, i.e. 7½ by 12½ of our inches according to Collier. It is said that they were remarkable for their intelligence and understood how to drag a horse by the bridle and to carry a torch in their mouths. These imported dogs outdid the Chinese dog in popularity; one of their colloquial names was 'ha pa' and another, according to Lauffer, was Shih Tzu Kou or 'lion dog'. 'Ha pa' was translated as 'pet' or 'lap' dog with short legs. Lauffer considered he could not authoritatively state how the dogs came to Turkey, but Collier writes that there are records to show the type was probably Maltese in origin, dogs from Malta having been imported to Turkey and become very popular there.

The 'pug' dogs of Shantung Province were also referred to as 'Turkish' and 'ha pa' dogs. In the description of the prefecture of Shan t'ien the following passage occurs: 'The long haired among them are designated "monkey-lion dogs" (*nae* = a long yellow-haired monkey). The people of the locality call it "Shih nung kou" (*nao, nung*, or *nang* = a fierce, shaggy-haired watch-dog).'

Reference is also made to H. Ramsay's *Western Tibet*, and Lauffer comments 'It is interesting to note that the Chinese pug-dogs were introduced as far as Lhasa. In Tibet they are called "Lags K'ye" (i.e. hand dogs) because it is believed that if a human being lays hands upon a young eagle when freshly hatched the bird is transformed into a dog of the Chinese pug breed.' As used here the word 'pug' could have been a purely literary translation.

Another 'pug' is, however, recorded in a work of the Sung Dynasty; this is the Lo-chiang dog, which comes from the Ssuch'uan Province. In A.D. 990–94 they were sent in tribute to the Emperor, and described as being very small, intelligent, always tame and docile; they sat beside the Imperial couch, and at every audience they were supposed to wag their tails and bark first so that people would be properly respectful. A later work, written at the end of the 11th century, mentions one of these dogs as in red colour. It is not clear to which 'pug dog' Ramsay refers when he says that the Chinese pug was exported as far as Lhasa.

Chinese Sleeve dogs

The height of the lap-dog cult was reached in the reign of Tao Kung (1821–51), at which time dwarf dogs were reared which had been cruelly stunted by artificial means. When large sleeves became fashionable these dogs (of various breeds) took the added name of sleeve dog. Collier, writing in 1921, says that this name was then unknown to dog fanciers in Peking, and the cult of

dwarfing had not existed for the past seventy years. The Empress
Dowager Tzu Hsi objected to the artificial dwarfing of such small
dogs, which were always in the nature of freaks.

Restriction of food was apparently one of the methods adopted
and another is said to have been the practice of enveloping small
puppies in wire cages closely fitting the body, which were not
removed until maturity.

Breeding

There were no written standards, but careful records were kept on
scrolls and by means of pictures in the dog books. The Emperors
and Empresses also had illustrations of their favourite dogs
painted by the court artist, and in these ways current fashions
were dictated to which the eunuchs would breed. The scroll
among my illustrations portrays the three Chinese breeds together,
the Pekingese, the Pug and the Shih Tzu; this is the rare type of
Shih Tzu which was bred in China.

It is reported that the eunuchs – numbering at least a thousand,
at one time reputed to be as many as four thousand, and living
in the 'Forty-eight places' in the Palace – would try to outdo each
other in breeding the best specimens. At this period the only
dogs obtainable from the Palace were the inferior specimens sold
in the market, but dog breeding is known to have been practised
in the homes of the people for hundreds of years.

According to Collier, a Chinese historian describing the
Imperial menagerie in the time of Kublai Khan remarked 'the
lions (which were kept in the Palace and paraded for the Imperial
guests) are of the same colour and astonishingly like the golden-
coated nimble dogs which are commonly bred by the people in
their homes'. Another reference made by a Chinese chronicler in
the same period says 'there was a civilian named Shen Heng Chi
who bred a "Chin Ssu" (literally "golden-silk") dog in his home.
This dog was not more than one foot long, and was very intelligent. When guests were presented the dog lay beneath the
table.'

The Empress Dowager was said to personally supervise as
many as a hundred dogs. According to Miss Carl – who lived in
the Chinese court for ten months – one of her great favourites
which followed her around was an animal of the long-coated

variety which the Empress called Tibetan, but she was not successful in breeding this type. Miss Carl also mentions that the Empress
was particularly interested in symmetrical marking, and like her
predecessor encouraged the lion dog appearance to perpetuate the
comparison between the Emperors and Buddha. In *Lhasa Lion
Dog* by Madame Lu Zee Yuen Nee there are various references
to the Shih Tzu being delicate and difficult to breed in the
Palace, and also to their difficulty in whelping. We have not
experienced this problem with our English stock, and in fact
Lady Brownrigg was always most anxious to preserve the breed's
ease of whelping.

According to Collier the Tibetan lion dogs existing when he
was in Peking were sometimes as diminutive as the common
Pekingese, but usually somewhat larger. He adds that Chinese
breeders distinguish two varieties, which is borne out by the
Chinese scroll and in paintings. There is the ordinary shock-
headed dog with hair standing out on the face and bridge of the
nose, and then the extremely rare 'nae y'ou' of which the forehead
only is shaggy, the lower parts of the face being short-haired; the
Chinese lion dogs (Shih Tzu Kou) are longer-nosed than the
flat-faced Pekingese. Collier also mentions that nowadays the
breed is sometimes crossed with Pekingese with a view to introducing length of coat into the latter. Many Chinese Pekes are
portrayed in scrolls as having short body hair, and do not have the
flat nose of our modern variety; also the mouth of the Shih Tzu
is drawn differently from that of the Peke. I find it surprising that
no reference is made to the 'rare Shih Tzu type' by foreigners in
China during the 1920s and 1930s. They must have been very
rare indeed – could they have become extinct?

The Chinese 'lion dog' is so called chiefly on account of the
length and shagginess of its coat. Many superstitions are held by
the Chinese regarding colours and markings – fortunate markings
could bring honour to a family, and every colour had its value.
Some of the thirty-two superior marks of Buddha were encouraged in the dogs, such as:

4) 'Between the eyebrows a little ball shining like silver or
snow' (the white top-knot).

12) 'The tongue large and long' (this was encouraged in the
early Peke, and it was customary to pull continually on the tongue

of a puppy to make it hang out, though this practice caused it to hang from the middle of the mouth instead of the side where it should have been).

13) 'The jaws those of the lion' (i.e. broad, as portrayed in their lions).

17) 'The skin having a tinge of gold colour' (yellow and gold-coated Shih Tzu were highly prized on this account).

The saddle marking was also prized, because of the connection with Buddha when he rode on the back of his transformed 'ha pa' dog.

The Comtesse d'Anjou was considered to be an authority on the breed in China, although it has been implied that she was only interested in tiny Shih Tzu, and that in the Imperial Palace no animals weighed more than 12 lb. According to Mrs. Audrey Fowler, 'In 1954 Count d'Anjou wrote out a standard of the breed for France, taken from the booklet by Madam Lu Zee Yuen Nee and approved by the French judge Monsieur Frick and Monsieur Chayet, who was a judge at dog shows in Peking, and states he was a breeder of half a hundred Shih Tzu. The Comtesse wrote a résumé of this standard for the newspaper *La Vie Canine Paris*; amongst other things she says, 'Regarding the assertion of rumours circulated that the Tibetan Shih Tzu are a Peke cross, this is utterly false, they are a pure breed originating from Tibet and were presented to the Emperors of China two or three hundred years ago.' With reference to weight, she refers to a standard weight of 5–10 kilos (i.e. 11 lb 3 oz–22 lb 9 oz), '*et même un peu plus*' (even a little more).

There are many other experts, including Dr. Walter Young (quoted in *This is the Shih Tzu*) and Madame Lu Zee Yuen Nee (*The Lhasa Lion Dog*), who consider the Shih Tzu to have been a pure breed in Tibet. There is a Tibetan pastel drawing (1932) of an indisputable gold and white Shih Tzu owned by Mrs. Olive Grindey, and also the reference of Lauffers (Ramsay) to 'dogs of the Chinese pug breed being exported as far as Lhasa', which could have accounted for the short nose.

It is, however, very likely that the longer nosed Apso was taken into India, which was no longer a strongly Buddhist country, for the dogs seen there are mostly of that type, and Sherpa Tensing owned about thirty at the time of the conquest of Everest. The shorter-nosed lion dogs were mainly sent to China, where this species was so highly valued.

Later Chinese

Following the death of the Empress Dowager Tzu Hsi in 1908, there was no one to supervise dog breeding in the Imperial Palace, for the puppet Emperor, Pu-Yi, was not interested in the Palace dogs; many of them were given away by the eunuchs to important Chinese families and high-ranking foreign officials, while others were sold in the dog markets of Lung Fu Ssu and Hu Kuo Ssu, both old Lamaist temples.

Dog breeding continued outside the Palace in both Chinese and foreign families; the lion dogs were jealously guarded and it was believed that the Chinese would go to great lengths to prevent live dogs and puppies from leaving the country. This was confirmed by Mrs. Audrey Fowler; when she handed her puppies into the care of the ship's butcher (which was obligatory) she was told 'Oh, they will only live a few days.' On asking 'Why?' she was told 'The Chinese always give these puppies powdered glass just before they leave as they do not want them to leave the country.' You can imagine how relieved she was that her puppies had not been bought from a Chinese family!

Breeding within the Palace continued to a lesser degree, for there are records of Palace dogs being given away as late as 1928. According to Easton in *This is the Shih Tzu*, all but fifty of the one thousand eunuchs were dismissed in 1923. Three Dowagers were left, one of whom died soon after the dismissal of the eunuchs, while the other two were turned out in 1924, some days before the flight of the Emperor to Tientsin.

From my own experience of breeding, and realising the changes which can be accomplished in a very short time, it is hard to understand why – at a time of great unrest and disturbance – Palace stock should have been thought superior to dogs bred outside the Palace, where breeding had also been carried on for hundreds of years.

We know from many people who were in China in the 'twenties and 'thirties, and also from Sowerby (Editor of the *Chinese Chronicle*, and a dog judge) that the Tibetan breeds were all grouped together under the following names:

Tibetan Poodle
Shih Tzu Kou (literal translation, Lion Dog)
Lhasa terrier
Apso
Ha pa or ha-par'rh kou
Lion Dogs

There was great confusion in distinguishing between the breeds, and this was eventually accomplished with the aid of the English Kennel Club, which had already divided the Tibetan breeds into their correct categories.

Sowerby told in the *Chinese Chronicle* of 1930 (*Manchu News Letter*) how he was a judge at the China Kennel Club show in Shanghai classifying 'the Lhasa Terrier or Tibetan Poodle'. It was no secret, he said, that he experienced considerable difficulty in deciding how to adjudicate, for there was no guiding information laid down concerning the breed; this is hardly surprising, for the breed would seem to have been wrongly named so far as the China Kennel Club was concerned. Mr. Sowerby continuously urged that the breeds should be clarified. In 1933, he described the difference between the Peke and the Apso by referring to the latter as having 'very long rather stiff outstanding hair (not a flat coat as in the Pekingese) all over the body, legs and face'. He goes on to say that crossing has been taking place, as some dogs, coming from Peking and winning prizes, on investigation had been the offspring of pure Pekingese bitches sired by so-called Tibetans.

In 1934 the Peking Kennel Club was formed, and in 1938 their standard was drawn up. According to Alan Roger (who knew her well) Madame de Breuil, a Russian refugee, was largely instrumental in drawing up the standard, and other owners involved included the Comtesse d'Anjou. The main points are given here:

Chinese standard 1938

Long Ears: Heart-shaped (the longer the hair on the ears the better).
Long Apron and Pantaloons: (long hair difficult to find on hind-legs and all the more appreciated).
Size: 13–18 in.

Weight: 10–15 lbs.

Height: 9–12 in.

Eyes: Large and clear (hair should fall over them and cover them completely if possible).

Toes: Well-feathered, paws broad and flat.

Front Legs: May be slightly bowed (controversy about this).

Hindquarters: Slightly higher than the back.

Hair: As glossy as possible; apron and pantaloons wavy.

Skull: Broad and flat.

Tail: Well-plumed, carried gaily over the back.

Colours: All colours permissible, single and mixed. Tawny or honey-coloured highly favoured.

Some eyewitness accounts of the Shih Tzu in Asia

Monsieur Graeffe (Belgian Minister at Teheran, Iran) and his wife had a number of Shih Tzu which they had brought from Peking, their previous post, between 1941 and 1945; these were seen by Alan Roger, and also by Mrs. Sheila Bode who later became an English breeder. Alan Roger remembers them as being brown and gold in colour, and it was acquaintance with these dogs that made him determined to own some himself when the war was over. Unfortunately this strain died out, but they varied in size and were probably 14–20 lb in weight.

Strangely enough, within three days of his arrival in Hong Kong after its liberation from the Japanese in 1945, he saw a small bedraggled dog rush out of the sea towards him, and recognised it as a Shih Tzu: the colouring was grey, white and black. The dog's master said he knew of no others in Hong Kong, this one having been saved from the Japanese by a faithful house boy in Shanghai, and brought from there after the end of the war.

After an interval of three years a dog puppy was acquired out of parents from Peking; he was almost pure white with apricot ears. Soon after this Alan Roger acquired a grey and white bitch from a Chinese who was returning to China (where pet dogs were not permitted by the Communist authorities), and wanted to find a satisfactory home for his much-loved pet.

The parents of the dog puppy were brought to Hong Kong by Mr. and Mrs. Harman, the former having been Consul-General in

Peking. It is believed that those dogs which were retained by the Harmans went with them to the U.S.A., and under the conditions prevailing at that time were no doubt metamorphosed into Apsos!

Dr. Nesfield, who was medical officer for the Younghusband expedition in 1904, wrote to Mrs. Fowler in February 1956 about the dog which was given to him by the Dalai Lama:

I cannot tell you how this dog originated. I know the breed is very old. I got mine in Lhasa in 1904 during the Younghusband expedition. She came back with me to India and died in Gemilet, Assam, in 1910 from fever. There is no dog I imagine more faithful and more affectionate. She would not go to anyone else. They are believed to bring good luck, hence the honour in receiving one. My dog came from the Dalai Lama, who at that time had fled from Lhasa. The thirteenth Dalai Lama gave these dogs as special gifts to the old Empress of China. That is why specimens are found in Peking. My dog is gold and white. The face was not like a Peke, i.e. stumpy.

Mrs. Fowler's interest in these dogs stems from Dr. Nesfield, who was her family doctor in Sussex, and it was his account of them which made her determined to obtain one herself. Whilst on a visit to friends in China during the winter of 1936–7, she tried in both Hong Kong and Shanghai without success; however, in Peking she met the Comtesse d'Anjou, from whom she was fortunate in obtaining a gold and white bitch puppy, also a little honey-coloured bitch from Miss Frances Beiber, who was a great authority on the myth of the sacred lion of Buddha. According to Mrs. Fowler a saying of the Chinese is that the Shih Tzu is 'An honoured member of the family with its head on the pillow'. She describes the dogs in a show held at Peking in 1936 as being of average size and various colours, although the golden ones were the most highly prized.

Another description, according to Gay Widdrington in *The Shih Tzu Handbook,* is written on a scroll depicting a parti-coloured Shih Tzu which according to the caption is 'From Tibet and very rare, its character is that of a human being'.

I have related the facts I have been able to ascertain, although I am sure there must be many more untapped sources of information which will eventually come to light. We may all form our own opinions as to the origin of this little dog, but I hope I have made it quite clear that it has always been regarded as an honoured member of the family, and I feel that it is only by treating it in this way, with love and respect, that the true character of the breed becomes known.

2

The Shih Tzu Comes to Europe

Great Britain – Pre-War

Although specimens of the breed had occasionally been brought into this country in the early part of the century – and even exhibited – no breeding took place here until Miss Hutchins brought in one pair of her own dogs and another pair belonging to General and Mrs. Douglas Brownrigg (later Sir Douglas and Lady Brownrigg).

In 1958, thirty years after the Brownriggs acquired their first Shih Tzu in China, Lady Brownrigg wrote an article on 'How it all began', in which she recounted the difficulty she had experienced in obtaining the good specimens she wanted. She saw many dogs which were too large and coarse, and these she was careful to avoid. Some resembled the Lhasa terriers she had seen at championship shows, and she felt convinced that they were a separate breed; in this she was quite correct, although it was some years before this was generally recognised and accepted.

By the time Miss Hutchins and the Brownriggs met and became friendly the former had already bought her dog, Lung Fu Ssu. It was seeing Miss Hutchins' dog which made Lady Brownrigg even more determined to possess her own.

The bitch Shu Ssa was the first to be found, and this is how Lady Brownrigg described her: 'She was white with a black patch on her side, root of tail and head. This (latter) had a white topknot or apple mark. Her hair was not as long as it became, but stuck up all round her face, and with her large eyes she looked like a fluffy baby owl or perhaps a chrysanthemum! She quickly enslaved us and was extremely clever!' The Shih Tzu is sometimes known as the 'Chrysanthemum' dog.

Two points which were always of particular importance to Lady Brownrigg were character and ease of whelping. She found her Shih Tzu even more intelligent and sporting than her standard poodle Ch. Polaire, who was gun-trained and a very good retriever.

A mate for Shu Ssa was subsequently found – Hibou, whose master (a French doctor) had returned home. Hibou, of a lighter build than either Shu Ssa or Miss Hutchins' Lung Fu Ssu, was described as 'very active, a great character and sportsman'. Shu Ssa was exceptionally fond of swimming, but Hibou did not like water! Shu Ssa had her first litter by Hibou in China.

Miss Hutchins returned to England in 1930, taking with her the Brownriggs' dog and bitch, her own Lung Fu Ssu and another bitch called Mei Mei. Unfortunately Mei Mei was killed by a sealyham after coming out of quarantine, but Shu Ssa's second litter was born while she was in quarantine. The Brownriggs returned to this country in 1931.

The weights of the early specimens were 12.1 lb, 13.10 lb and 14.9 lb. This was the ideal weight and size range so far as Lady Brownrigg was concerned; she did see some very small animals, and was well aware that a different range existed in China, but said that the very small dogs were not used for breeding.

It was at about the same time that Colonel and Mrs. Eric Bailey imported several dogs from the border of Tibet, calling them Apsos. The Brownrigg dogs were still called Tibetan Lion Dogs, the name most frequently used in China. When the Brownriggs went to see two of the Baileys' dogs, they 'found that apart from colour (they were brown or golden and one black) they had narrower heads, longer noses and smaller eyes than our dogs.' However, the Shih Tzu were accepted into the ranks of the Apsos, the Apso and Lion Dog Club was later formed, and they were recognised by the Kennel Club. When first shown alongside the Apsos in 1933 at the West of England Ladies Kennel Society championship show, it was realised that they were quite distinct breeds and in 1934 it was ruled by the Tibetan Breed Association that the Tibetan Lion Dogs which the Brownriggs had imported were in fact a separate breed.

In consultation with Mr. Croxton-Smith, a prominent member of the Kennel Club at that time, it was decided to adopt the Chinese name for the breed, Shih Tzu, and in September 1934 the application to change the title of the Apso and Lion Dog Club to Shih Tzu (Tibetan Lion Dog) Club was granted. In 1935 this was finally altered to the Shih Tzu Club.

At this point complete co-operation existed between Miss Hutchins and the Brownriggs over the breeding of the Shih Tzu in England. Minute details of every new puppy were supplied, and each available litter was inspected; any pups which did not conform to the highest standards were either not registered or were sold as pets.

The Club went from strength to strength, with General Brownrigg as Treasurer and his wife as Secretary, and registrations were increasing. The total up to the end of 1939 was 183, and there were forty-seven new registrations during that year. Two bitches were exported to the U.S.A. in 1938, to be re-registered there as Apsos. Amoy – by Yangtze out of Tzu Hsi – was exported to Mr. Walter Ekman in Sweden in 1935 and lived to be twenty-one. Mr. Ekman subsequently became the Swedish Consul-General in Holland, and after the war Lady Brownrigg visited the family and saw Amoy in good health.

There were other imports before the war, but unfortunately most of these lines died out. Imports included:

Hitsui   by Mrs. R. Bourke-Burrowes.

Taragul   by Mrs. B. Manico-Gull.

Ping Erh   by Mrs. Hull.

Dol Ma   (breeder Madame Wilden) by Hon. J. Hare and Hon. J. Fox-Strangeways. Although there were two litters here, the line died out.

My Lord of Tibet   (breeder Mme Kauffmann) by Lady Constance Butler. Descendants could be in Ireland, as there were two litters ex Ah Tishoo of Way (Tumbler).

*Choo Choo   half-brother to the above, imported to Queen Elizabeth.

*Tashi of Chouette   (breeder Mrs. Morgan, Canada), by Lady Brownrigg and Miss Reoch; also two dogs, who died. The bitch Tashi went to Lord Essex.

Fu Tzu Niu San   (breeder Comtesse d'Anjou) brought from China by Mrs. Audrey Fowler in 1937, but left no progeny.

*Ming   from China by Mrs. Telfer-Smollett in 1939; also a dog and two of their puppies which died in quarantine.

At the outbreak of war in September 1939 activities ceased, and there were no more imports until hostilities ended.

* Lines which have been continued.

Tashi Lhumpo.
Registered at the
Calcutta Kennel
Club. Exhibited
Cruft's 1909

Lady Brownrigg
with a group of her
early Shih Tzu

Hibou, Yangtze, Yo
Fei and Tzu Hsi,
1934

'Dogs at Play.' Section of Chinese scroll, owned by Mr. Alan Roger, showing a Pug, Shih Tzu, and a Pekingese

(Alison Snell)

'The Conversation Piece.' Mr. Alan Roger with Golden Da-Fung and Golden Go Kai Kun. Oil painting by John Ward, R.A., exhibited at the Royal Academy Summer Exhibition, 1955

In 1939 Mee Na of Taishan was sold to Mrs. Garforth Bless (later Mrs. Widdrington) as a non-show specimen, being on the large side and having uneven markings over her eyes. Although the bitch was too large it was always made clear that tiny or toy dogs were not desirable. Mee Na became the foundation bitch of the Lhakang Kennel, which has had an important influence on the breed.

During pre-war years the Club sponsored classes at many championship shows, and dogs were extensively shown in 'any other variety' categories in Scotland and England. The breed always attracted a great deal of attention.

Lady Brownrigg sought out every import she heard about, and inspected and advised on as many puppies as was practicable. Details of whelping and puppies were sent to her, and it is interesting that although no mention is made of difficult whelpings, there was a high mortality rate amongst the puppies. It was doubtless careful culling (plus the loss of the weaker puppies because veterinary science was not then so advanced) which kept the breed so strong, for there were no signs of weakness caused by inbreeding.

Enquiries came from all over the world. In China, matters were confused, for the breeds had not been distinguished and were judged together without any standard. It was not until after our standard had been drawn up in England that the Peking Kennel Club was formed in 1934, and standards were then drawn up for the various dogs.

In 1940 the breed was granted a separate register, having been registered under 'Any other Variety' since 1932; it now became eligible for Challenge Certificates, but none were actually awarded until after the war.

During the war years, Lady Brownrigg was very busy with Red Cross work, and breeding practically ceased. Wool from the grooming of the dogs' coats was made into yarn, and used for knitting articles which were sold in aid of the Red Cross. Between 1940 and 1967 registrations dwindled to a total of sixty-one.

Great Britain – Post-War

After the war Mrs. Garforth-Bless (Widdrington) helped Lady Brownrigg to get the Club back on its feet; they acted as Treasurer

C

and Secretary respectively, and the future outlook for the breed was hopeful.

Imports in this immediate post-war period included:

Ishuh Tzu from China in 1948 by Major-General Telfer-Smollett.
Pjokken Dux from Norway in 1948 by Mrs. Widdrington.
Jungfältets Jung Ming from Sweden by Mrs. Longden.
Hsi Li Ya from China in 1952 by Mrs. Dobson.
Wuffles and *Mai-ting* imported in 1948 and 1949, but not incorporated into our lines until 1962 when this was achieved through a grand-daughter Gun-yiang of Lunghwa (Gay Widdrington: *Shih Tzu Handbook*).

The first champion, Ta Chi of Taishan, was made up in 1949; she was liver and white, and came through on the imported lines of Swedish Choo Choo and Canadian Tashi of Chouette as well as our original lines. She was a very fine specimen of the breed, and is even now considered to be the type to aim for by most of the knowledgeable breeders in this country.

Lady Brownrigg remained Secretary of the Shih Tzu Club until 1954, when she became President, and was still taking a very active interest in the breed when she died in April 1969. The Hon. Mrs. Bruce – her childhood friend – is still our patron. The latter obtained her Shih Tzu from the earliest litters, and was influential in encouraging the breed in Scotland. Her beautiful Sungari, by Hibou out of Shu Ssa, came from the first litter born out of quarantine, and would not look out of place in the show ring today.

The advent of the 1950s brought new breeders and many changes. The Antarctica kennel of Mr. and Mrs. K. B. Rawlings entered the Shih Tzu show ring in 1950 with Perky Ching of the Mynd; this kennel brought a vast improvement in coats and general show ring presentation. In 1951 Miss Freda Evans, of the Elfann kennel, who was a highly successful Peke breeder, acquired Fenling of Yram – later Elfann Fenling of Yram – bred by Mrs. Haycock.

During this decade, top show honours in the breed went mainly to the three kennels of Taishan, Lhakang and Antarctica. However, there were also a great many other good dogs belonging to smaller kennels which were limited in their showing and therefore did not have so great a chance to make up champions.

The Taishan Kennel bred only one litter of importance in the 1950s; this was by Ch. Choo Ling out of Ch. Pa Ko of Taishan, and following a bad start with distemper, this litter produced three champions. One was English Ch. Wang Poo of Taishan, whose smaller brother Pei Ho won two C.C.s and two reserve C.C.s in England before being taken to Australia as foundation stock by his owners, Mr. and Mrs. Dobson; here he became an Australian Champion. The third brother was exported to Italy, where he also became a champion. After this Taishan faded out of the breeding programme, only having one more litter in 1962 in an effort to obtain a bitch from her own line for Lady Langman.

The latter was the owner of Fu of Taishan – the only bitch mated to the Queen's Choo Choo – and had written to Lady Brownrigg to say how attached she had been to 'Fu' and how she would dearly love another. This spurred Lady Brownrigg, with my co-operation, into mating a daughter of Ch. Wang Poo of Taishan, who was grandson to Li Ching Chao. The bitch was whelped at my home, where Lady Brownrigg stayed with me and had the dam in her room that night. Whelping certainly did not seem too far off, but in the short time whilst Lady Brownrigg was having her bath two puppies were born, so quietly that she was still unaware there were any until the third pup squeaked! There was one bitch in the litter of six which was similar to Fu of Taishan – named Fu Wang, she was earmarked for Lady Langman although not quite the pick of the litter. Lady Brownrigg delayed the puppies' departure for as long as possible, which in Lady Langman's case was unfortunately too long for, unhappily she died just before Fu Wang was permitted to go to her. The remainder of the litter eventually went to old friends and families of early breeders, but I do not think any of them were used for breeding, so unfortunately the line has died out. Fu Wang was the biggest escapist we have ever known, and was named 'the devil dog'; when Lady Brownrigg died she and her dam – the only ones left in the kennel – came to live with me, and even now at rising ten years of age she is still a remarkable escapist!

Referring back to the changes in the 1950s which I mentioned, there was a period which caused so much trouble and unhappiness within the Club and breed that I would gladly have left it un-

recorded, but as this is a true history of the breed I feel it must
be set down.

The Peke Cross, 1952

Miss Freda Evans, a Peke breeder of high repute and breeder of
many champions, had come into the breed in 1951. She considered that certain faults were creeping in, and specified 'over-
size, narrow heads, over-long noses and snipey muzzles, terrier
legs with narrow fronts, loose jointedness, poor coats, small
near-set eyes and bad carriage'. What a depressing picture this
conjures up! There were some extremely fine specimens around
at that time, according to show reports and pictures! However,
Mrs. Widdrington, who had recently imported a Shih Tzu which
had left no progeny, wrote that she considered the cross would
bring in fewer faults than an imported Shih Tzu of unknown
pedigree.

The crossing of the Shih Tzu to the Peke at that time would
not necessarily have been a bad thing for the breed if the faults
mentioned above really had become prominent, but this was
disputed by many other breeders. The fact that this crossing was
undertaken by a newcomer into the *breed*, however experienced,
and without prior consultation with the Breed Club whose main
object was to protect and improve standards, caused untold
trouble for years to come. It was not until after the puppies of
the first cross were born that a letter was written explaining the
motives involved. Lady Brownrigg did not give her approval,
although she did permit her Ch. Choo Ling to be used on the
bitch of the first cross. We cannot tell whether this was in order
to make the best of a bad situation, or whether she would have
been in agreement had she been consulted beforehand.

It cannot be sufficiently strongly emphasised that *nobody* should
ever undertake such a step again. The modern Peke does not
resemble the original Chinese Peke, and there would in fact be
more attributes to breed out than in. Present-day Pekes with their
exaggerated features and totally different build, complete lack
of nose (which is situated up between the eyes), can do nothing
but harm to our healthy and active little Shih Tzu. We do not
want dogs with noses which are too short, for this can cause
many problems to health; neither do we want the noses set too

Peke cross pedigree

3rd gen cross

Michelcombe Dinkums
Ti-Ni-Tim of Michelcombe

Mu-Ho
Shih-Wei-Tzu

Fu Chuan of Elfann
- Ch. Hong of Hungjao
  - Pu of Oulton
  - Sing Pu
- Chuanne Tu of Elfann
  - Wu Chow of Shuanghsi
  - Elfann Fenling of Yram

2nd gen cross
Yu Honey of Elfann
- Ch. Choo Ling
  - Sanus Ching-A-Boo
  - Sing-Pu
- *1st gen cross*
  Ye Sunny of Elfann
  - Philadelphus Suti-T'sun of Elfann (*Peke*)
  - Elfann Fenling of Yram

high, for the hair of the Shih Tzu (which grows up on the nose) can cause eye trouble. We do not want the bowed legs; many of the early dogs did have this feature thrown through Shu Ssa, but it was being bred out. The Shih Tzu's elbow is ideally on a level with the brisket line, and the shoulders lie close to the rib cage. I appeal to all would-be 'experimenters' to leave the breed alone, and if you should feel that there is room for improvement, please bring this to the notice of the Breed Clubs concerned.

The Peke chosen was a championship show-winning specimen, reddish-fawn and white, selected because of his rather straight legs and level jaw, excellent dark pigment and large eyes. The dam was Elfann Fenling of Yram, a nice type of Shih Tzu bitch descended from two champions (Choo Ling and Shebo Tsemo of Lhakang). This cross was correctly registered with the Kennel Club. In each succeeding generation, one bitch puppy only was mated back to a Shih Tzu, until the third generation – still cross-breed – when six puppies were registered, four of which were bred from. The progeny of these matings were eligible for first-class registrations as pure Shih Tzu. The names of the third-generation crosses were:

Ti-ni-tim of Michelcombe (d)   transferred to Mrs. Widdrington in the north of England, who also had *Michelcombe Pee-Kin-Pus* (b).
Elfann Shih Wei Tzu (b)   transferred to Mrs. Murray Kerr, a Scottish breeder.
Mu Ho (d)   transferred to Mrs. Thelma Morgan in the Midlands.
Michelcombe Fucia (b) and *Michelcombe Dinkums* (b)   remained with Miss O. I. Nichols of Devon, who had the dam Yu Honey (cross-breed).

From the above, the dogs Ti-ni-Tim and Mu ho and the bitches Michelcombe Dinkums and Shih Wei Tzu were used for breeding.

Extensive breeding then went ahead, the animals being so well distributed throughout the country that in a few years it became difficult to find sufficient stock without this line in order to avoid inbreeding. Consequently the majority of kennels have this line in their animals, although there are still some without it.

Cross or no cross, the dogs of 1973 – twenty years after the cross was first perpetrated – are much more uniform in size; the

larger type which had earlier become too big is seldom seen in
the show ring nowadays. In the main, the smaller size is not now
much below 12 lb, and of good solid type, well constructed.
Both the Swedish and the Peke lines helped to reduce the overall
size. The most difficult Peke feature to breed out was the over-
bowed front, and in too many instances this still persists.
Personally, I blame this on the heavy coats (which disguise what
is underneath) and clever handling in the show ring, allied with
the fact that when 'straight' legs were deleted from the standard in
1953 nothing was inserted as a guide for judges and breeders.

According to Burns and Fraser, the achondroplastic (short-leg)
gene – as in the Peke – affects heavy bone more than fine bone,
making it more difficult to get a short-legged dog with straight
legs if the bone is heavy than if it is light, '. . . heavy bone being
soft, bends more easily, and is also more liable to inherited
rickets'. There has never been anything in the Shih Tzu standard
to state that the bone should be heavy, only 'muscular with
ample bone, and should look massive on account of the wealth
of hair'. On the other hand, too fine a bone, which is inclined to be
thrown from our Swedish line, is not desirable either – it is quite
possible to obtain a medium thickness.

After this upheaval over the Peke cross, another was to follow,
when the Lhakang Kennel began to specialise in breeding 'tinies'.
At an Annual General Meeting the interested parties won a
majority vote to have the weight altered to 'up to 18 lb, ideal
weight 9–16 lb'. Coming after the schism of opinion over the
Peke cross, this split the Club and breed in two.

The principal objection to breeding miniatures was that this
would produce a toy breed and cause unnecessary suffering
during whelping, whereas one of the main features of the breed
had always been ease of whelping. Also, so many breeds have
come near to ruin due to breeding down in size. Had some
provision been made in the standard for a minimum weight of
even 9 lb – though 10 lb was more likely to have been acceptable
– all might even then have been well. Lady Brownrigg wrote to
the Kennel Club, imploring them not to allow such a small size in
the breed; the Kennel Club disallowed miniatures, but permitted
'tinies' and accepted the revised standard. Lady Brownrigg then
asked if there could not be a division into two sizes, but this was
refused on the grounds that numerically the breed was too small.

Provision was then made for the lower size range, and weight classes were then put on at shows to accommodate the smaller dogs; these classes were guaranteed by the Shih Tzu Club, which for many years sustained a sad loss in this respect. However, in 1971 the standard was altered to impose a minimum limit, i.e. '10–18 lb, ideal 10–16 lb'.

In 1956 a private club was started by Mrs. Longden to encourage the small size. Application was made to the Kennel Club for the right to have its own title, but since the aims of the Club were 'to foster a small size', this was not granted. Eventually in 1962, on the intervention of Owen Grindey (later Chairman), the aims of the Club were changed to 'to promote and protect the breed and preserve it on the right lines according to the Kennel Club standard of 1958'. The same official standard was also to be used. The Manchu Shih Tzu Club was now officially in being, with Mrs. Widdrington as President, Mrs. Bode as Secretary and Owen Grindey as Chairman.

This is all past history now, but none the less it forms a vital part of the breed's progress and had to be recounted. At this time the breed is going from strength to strength and the two Clubs are friendly and co-operative, largely due to the guidance of Owen Grindey. Both Clubs cater well for their members by giving all the help they can, in newsletters, rallies and teach-ins. Breeding is on a very sound basis, the majority of breeders aiming for the 12–15 lb size. Provided breeders are not blind to the faults in their own stock (for few dogs are without fault) the breed should remain in a most healthy state for years to come.

There is little more to add in order to bring the breed right up to date.

In 1958 Mrs. Longden exported Fu Ling of Clystvale to Mrs. Jungefeldt in Sweden, where he became a leading stud. In exchange she sent Mrs. Longden Jungfältets Jung Ming. There will be more about this line in the chapter on lines and families later in the book.

The advent of the 1960s saw the breed going ahead well. Registrations rose from 540 in 1967 to 1,526 in 1971. Exports also increased from 113 in 1967 to 554 in 1970, the majority going to the United States. Over 100 animals were exported to Japan between 1967 and 1969; while we have every sympathy for the heartbreak experienced by the unsuspecting breeder when the conditions then existing were realised, no good breeder or dog lover can feel anything but contempt for those whose one motive was a quick cash return. It should be placed on record that few of these exporters were regular breeders of this enchanting dog, though some regrettably were. Britain is supposed to be a country of dog lovers, and many of us felt deeply ashamed of some of our compatriots at that time. Unfortunately this can be the price paid by any breed when it gains popularity, and it is sad to reflect that the prospect of financial gain can cause people to act in such a way.

Now, in the 1970s, Ireland is well back in the picture, rapidly going from strength to strength with a total of four Irish Champions. There are two dog champions, owned by Mrs. Pearl Reynolds (Hollybough) and bred by Mrs. Olive Newson – Hollybough T'sing Hwa of Telota and Hollybough Heven of Telota. The other two champions are owned by Mrs. Hickey (Lyre) – one bitch bred by Mrs. Diana Harding, Taonan Tasmin of Lyre, and also Hi Fi of Lyre, home bred.

Norway

Dogs were imported into Norway in 1932 by Henrik Kauffmann, then Danish Minister to China, and his wife. They were the brown female Leidza, black and white bitch Schander*, and black and white dog Aidze. In 1933 Queen Maud of Norway brought one of the Kauffmanns' puppies to England for the Duchess of York (later Queen Elizabeth, now the Queen Mother). Letters which passed between Madame Kauffmann and Lady Brownrigg in 1934 show exactly how the Kauffmanns obtained their dogs. Madame Kauffmann knew that the Shih Tzu had been accepted as a separate breed in England, and that a standard was being fixed; she wrote:

Dear Mrs. Brownrigg,
    I was much interested in your letter and the photographs of your dogs. There is a light coloured dog in one of your pictures, I believe called Tai Tai – I wonder whether it is brown or white? – they all look so beautifully brushed. Tzu Hsi looks especially good, isn't she?
    I am also much in favour of getting a standard fixed for them –

* Although this dog is spelt Schander by the Kennel Club, it is referred to as Schauder by the Kennel Clubs of Norway and the U.S.A.

particularly because I believe one of mine to be among the very best of her kind either in China or in Europe.

We got our three in Peking. Our brown bitch, whom you see in the snapshot, was bought from an old palace eunuch and I know her to be from the palace stock. The black and white male, also begging, took me a year and a half to find, having seen dozens of dogs – because he is just as small as the brown one. For that reason I think he must come of good stock too, and had perhaps been stolen or given away – but I really know nothing about him.

Two years later we found the other little female, also black and white, having again had trouble about the size. I think she is not quite so good, being a bit higher from the ground, but not bad. She is in the background of the snow picture.

Madame Kauffmann continues by commenting on the number of people who have said the brown bitch is so good, says that she is adopting her as a criterion, and adds:

. . . so far none of her puppies have been quite her equal, unless a little black and white one I recently sent to London. I have just sent another one to England to Lady Constance Butler, which has a white spot on the nose. [This was My Lord of Tibet.]

I have a Chinese amah with me here who has been much interested in the dogs always, and she has learned a lot about Chinese standards in regard to them and told it to me. I wonder whether you have ever met a Mrs. Bailey who bought something like twelve dogs at Lung Fu Ssu within a few days and took them back to England to breed?

My Lord of Tibet, who was prominent at shows in 1936 and 1939, was used at stud to Ah Tishoo of Way (Tumbler). The line may have died out subsequently, or there may still be descendants in Ireland. My Lord of Tibet's sire was Law-Hu II, a son of Aidze and Schander. Incidentally, it is interesting here to note that Spratts' boarding charges in 1934 were 12/6d per week (62½p)! The price of a good Shih Tzu specimen was £20, and the first prize at a championship show was £2, the same as in 1971! In 1939 Crufts paid £2.10s. as a 1st Prize. With boarding kennel fees now costing as much per *day*, illustrating the terrific rise in the cost of food, wages, etc., and entry fees to show now at £1·50, one wonders how they could have made a show pay in the past. (Since first drafting this chapter, championship fees have risen to £2.)

THE SHIH TZU COMES TO EUROPE

Choo Choo, who was imported to our Duchess of York, was a son of the original imported pair from China, Aidze and Schander. When the Duchess became Queen, she gave Choo Choo into the care of her brother, the Hon. David Bowes-Lyon, and in 1937 he was with Lady Strathmore. He was mated to Lady Langman's Fu of Taishan, and the ensuing litter was reared by Lady Langman at North Cadbury Court, Yeovil. Mrs. Bowes-Lyon was most interested in Choo Choo's puppies and came to visit them; one went to Princess Margaret, although Princess Elizabeth spoke of him as hers. The bitch Li Ching Chao figures in all pedigrees.

At this time the dogs were still registered in Norway as Lhasa Terrier, the name they had had in China, but in 1939 the Norsk Kennel Club wrote to Lady Brownrigg as follows:

Some years ago Mrs. Kauffmann imported some dogs we here call Lhassa terrier from China, where she had stayed some years. One of these dogs was brought by our Queen to the Duchess of York, now Queen Elizabeth.

As we have some of these dogs left here, I would appreciate very much to know what you call these dogs in England.

Could you be so kind as to forward to us the standard for Lhassa terrier and the Shih Tzu?

An important distinction regarding the Kauffmann imports appears to have been concerning the jaws. Where puppies were exported by Madame Kauffmann with 'slightly undershot jaws' she mentioned this as a fault. However, in a later letter dated 1937, she wrote 'I must write and explain that none of my dogs have receding lower jaws – what you call "even" was what I called "receding" because the lower teeth fit in behind the upper ones.'

In June 1936 Madame Kauffmann wrote that one of her dogs 'died in March, just before she was to have puppies. I think the poor thing had too many puppies, but it seemed absolutely unpreventable. The only bitch I have left now is the honey-coloured one who is at least ten years old, so I don't think she will have any more.'

It should be appreciated that notes were regularly compared between the Kauffmanns and the Brownriggs, Madame Kauffmann having a great respect for Lady Brownrigg's opinion, and

it was mainly through the latter's intervention that the breed
ever became registered as Shih Tzu in Norway. Both had chosen
their imports with the greatest care; Lady Brownrigg had not
wanted the smaller Swedish dogs since, according to her, the
very tiny ones had not been bred from in the Imperial Palace in
China. It was not until Madame Kauffmann returned from China
that she became seriously interested in the breed.

3
Lines and Families

WITH every fresh line, fresh genes can bring good and bad traits, although it is not considered that these ancestral influences persist after the fourth generation. Since recessives can be carried for many generations, it is useful to know the origins of the various lines. At the same time it is up to every serious breeder to find out as much as possible about all the dogs in a four-generation pedigree, i.e. size, colour, character, action and other points necessary to make up a good dog. Genetics can be a considerable help, but this is a very young science, and genes do not fall neatly into either the dominant or recessive categories. All breeders should have some knowledge of Mendel's Law, and a good book which can be easily understood is Eleanor Frankling's *The Dog Breeder's Introduction to Genetics*.

Reading a pedigree does not only involve knowing the champions. Everyone who shows dogs realises that no animal is perfect – it is possible for a dog to gain its championship undeservedly, conversely many good specimens who deserve the honour are never able to achieve it. For to make a champion in England involves travelling to as many championship shows as possible, keeping the dog in top condition, frequently spending much more than one can afford, and above all rearing it correctly. A potential champion may be ruined through incorrect rearing, but unless this is due to wrong feeding it will not be prevented from throwing quality puppies.

Many people wonder why the breed is not completely uniform in type, though this is certainly much more so now than formerly. Selective breeding virtually ceased in China after the death of the Empress Tzu-hsi in 1908, and although dogs were chosen with care by both English and Swedish importers, the original animals were not entirely identical in body structure. There was some divergence in type, certainly in China, which was not only noticeable in general structure but also in size. While there was little variation in the actual size of our imported dogs, they threw both large and small puppies. Popen and Ting, both very tiny, were bred by Lady Brownrigg in the first litter in quarantine; these went to her parents and were not bred from. Changes in environment and improved feeding helped to increase the size, which is the main reason for the insertion in the standard of 'Type and breed characteristics of the greatest importance and on no account to be sacrificed to size alone'.

Although the early imports are now some forty years behind us, and of course so intermingled that it would be practically impossible to distinguish the lines if one wanted to, it is useful to know some of the points, particularly the hidden recessives, which could easily crop up again. Two which come to my mind are a white patch round one eye, and a too tight tail. Both are blamed on the Swedish line of Jungfältets Jung Ming, which does indeed perpetuate them, but many of our English lines are also carrying them since both faults were apparent long before Jungfältets Jung Ming was born.

The following is a description of the early imports whose lines have been continued, as recounted to me by Lady Brownrigg:

Shu Ssa (b).   Weight 12 lb 2 oz. White and black, predominantly white. She was the smallest of the three, rather more 'Pekey' in type. Her tail was rather too tight over her back. Good dark eyes and good square jaw. Imported 1930.
Hibou (d).   Weight 13 lb 10 oz. Black and white. Lighter in bone and higher on the leg than Shu Ssa. Very good tail, carried well over his back, good large head, nice jaw. Imported 1930.
Lung Fu Ssu (d).   Black and white, weight 14 lb 9 oz. A coarser coat which was inclined to be wavy. A good head, his tail was on the looser side. Imported 1930.
Choo Choo (d).   Black and white, but when young had brown colouring as well. His parents were smaller than he; he had too long a nose, with overshot jaw. Imported 1933 from Sweden.
Tashi of Chouette (b).   A small white and brown bitch, she brought in the chocolate colour. Imported 1938 from Canada.
Ming (b).   Black and white, a very nice specimen. Imported 1939.
Ishuh Tzu (b). Dark solid colour; the blacks came through on this

line, also solid clear golds. This line was the first to bring in the
solid colouring. Imported 1948.

Hsi-Li-Ya (b). According to Widdrington, she brought in a
pretty pale gold and white which seemed less recessive than the
red-gold and could be brought out by breeding to pastel grey.
Nostrils, which were inclined to be getting tight in the breed,
were improved by this line, as was the pigment.

Jung fältets Jung Ming (d). Black and white. Excellent coat, an
intelligent and gentle temperament. Good pigment, nostrils and
eyes. (There will be more about this line later.) An exceptionally
sweet, gentle and intelligent temperament, but some of his
progeny lacked boldness.

Lunghwa line. According to Widdrington (*Shih Tzu Handbook*)
this was from Wuffles and Mai-ting (imported in 1948 and 1949),
and was not incorporated into the main line of English stock
until 1962, through a black and white bitch – Gun-yiang of
Lunghwa – which was a grand-daughter of the original pair. This
line brought in a dense, lasting black and white with occasional
fawn shades from Wuffles. Puppies were often born with complete pigment. This is a sound and intelligent line with plenty
of natural instinct, but length of nose had to be watched in early
generations.

A dog or bitch can be outstanding for its show quality or for its
breeding quality. Frequently both are combined, but this is not
always so. A dog has a far better chance of being labelled as
influential than has a bitch, for it has greater opportunities to
beget the most puppies, and for a stud dog to be outstanding it
needs to sire good stock to many, and even to some indifferent,
bitches. A mediocre bitch can appear to be outstanding when she
produces fine puppies to an outstanding dog, but if she can
produce good puppies to indifferent dogs then her good influence
is manifest. Most of the credit invariably goes to the dog
rather than to the bitch, but then he usually gets any blame
too!

Since this book is about dogs rather than their breeders or
owners, I must be forgiven for mentioning so few kennels and
individuals. There are many excellent small kennels, which do
not have the same opportunities to achieve fame as the larger
establishments, but they continue to produce sound quality

stock. Most kennels in this breed are not very large, since the amount of attention required by the Shih Tzu makes it impracticable to keep large numbers.

Some influential dogs

Chen Fei (b). Bred by the Earl of Essex, she distinguished herself by going best of all breeds at a wartime City and Suburban show. She was a daughter of the imported Tashi of Chouette, sired by Jung Lo, a son of the original imports Lung Fu Ssu ex Shu Ssa. Tashi, as mentioned earlier, was imported by Lady Brownrigg and Miss Reoch, and later went to Lord Essex. Chen Fei was the grand dam of Ch. Ta Chi of Taishan; black and white herself, she carried the chocolate colouring.

Hsueh Li Chan of Taishan (b). Mated back to her sire Yangtze, she gave us the lovely dog Ch. Yu Mo Chuang of Boydon, who sired four champions in one litter to the bitch Ch. Mao Mao, and another – Ch. Pako of Taishan – when mated to Ch. Sing Tzu of Shebo.

Ch. Shebo Tsemo of Lhakang (d). Born in 1948, he was by Pu of Oulton out of Lindi Lu of Lhakang, and bred by Mrs. Widdrington. His early colour was red/brindle/white, later changing to grey/white, and has been a very strong champion line in the Antarctica kennels of Mr. and Mrs. Rawlings, particularly on the male side. Tsemo produced two champions, the bitch Ch. Shu-ssa of Michelcombe out of Chuanne Tu of Elfann, and a dog Ch. Yi Ting Mo of Antarctica – who headed a long line of champions – to the bitch Tang of Oulton. This line continued tail male in the Antarctica kennel, giving us his grandson Ch. Pan Wao Chen of Antarctica who made history in the breed by going Best in Show at W.E.L.K.S. in 1963. Then followed his great-grandson Ch. Fleeting Yu Sing, great-great-grandson Ch. Ya Tung of Antarctica, and great-great-great-grandson Ch. Kuire Hermes, the latter coming through on the Telota line of Mrs. Newson as a grandson of Ch. Domese of Telota. The first three champions of my own breeding also come through on Tsemo's line, namely Ch. Sindi Lu of Antarctica, a grand-daughter, Ch. Li Ching Ku of Snaefell and Ch. Su si of Snaefell, a grandson and grand-daughter respectively. Another Australian Ch. Hia Nan of Snaefell, is also a grand-daughter.

First Norwegian imports: Leidza with Schander in the background.

My Lord of Tibet, 1936. Half-brother of Choo Choo owned by HRH Duchess of York

(Ralph Robinson)

Hooza, grand-dam of Tashi of Chouette

Mrs. Audrey Fowler with Niu San and Fu Tzu returning to Britain on the *Empress*, 1937

The Hon Mrs. Robert Bruce with Sungari and Pie Ping, 1939

(Northern Photo Service)

Wen Shu of Lhakang (d). Bred by Mrs. Widdrington, and the first influential dog from the Peke cross line, he was the fourth generation, and the first to be given a first-class registration. He sired Ch. Choo Choo of Cathay and Ch. Shebo Wen Yin of Lhakang, and was instrumental in improving the quality of many of his progeny.

Choo Choo and *Ten Sing of Telota*. Some remarkably good stock has come through these two dogs, both owned by Mrs. Newson and bred by Miss Gill and Mrs. Newson respectively. Choo Choo's sire was Lundhouse Pong and the dam was Coral of Airlea. Ten Sing was sired by Tackla Sahib from the dam Chin Shih of Elfann. The famous Ch. Greenmoss Chin-Ki of Meo is a grandson of Choo Choo, and another well-known name is Ch. Tensing of Shanretta, a grandson of Ten Sing of Telota. One little bitch who always put her stamp on her puppies, no matter who sired them, was Domese of Telota who should really be given credit for starting a line of her own! She produced Ch. Dominic of Telota and Ch. Don Juan of Telota, also two Irish Champions, and the leading Canadian Champion in 1972 was Ch. Choo Lang of Telota. Ch. Kuire Hermes of Antarctica is a grandson of Domese.

Ch. Greenmoss Chin-Ki of Meo, bred by Mrs. V. Reynolds and owned by Mr. and Mrs. Leadbitter, must be the most famous stud in the breed, and has certainly been the most prolific. To the bitch Tricina Ky Lin (bred by Miss D. M. Bridge) he sired three champions in one litter: Ch. Sue Lin of Bridgend (b), Ch. Tricina Wen Mo of Bridgend (b) and Ch. Zeus of Bridgend (d). The breeders were Mr. and Mrs. Eric Carter. To Mei Lu Lu of Windtoi (bred by Mrs. Roberts) came Ch. Katrina of Greenmoss, bred by Mr. and Mrs. Leadbitter. Then there was Ch. Ching Ling of Greenmoss (bred by Mrs. J. Mangle) to the bitch Hsiang-chieh of Leddersdale (bred by Mrs. N. R. Parsons), and coming right up to date, Ch. Newroots Nankipoo of Snaefell (bred by Miss Fenner and Miss Thomas) to their bitch Ho Yan of New-roots*.

Ch. Chin-Ki, sired by Choo T'sun of Telota ex Elfann Maya Wen of Ricksoo, is a grandson of Choo Choo of Telota previously mentioned, and on the dam's side is also grandson to the famous Ch. Ellingham Kala Nag; the latter must have done more

* Since this chapter was written two sons, two daughters and two grand-daughters have become champions (*See* Appendix C).

D

big winning than any other dog in the breed under the expert handling of his owner, Mrs. Jean Lovely (he was bred by Lady Haggerston).

Other lines of interest are Int. Ch. Golden Peregrin of Elfann (bred by Miss E. M. Evans and exported to Italy by Mr. Leadbitter after winning his title), and Ch. Jen Kai Ko of Lhakang (bred by Mrs. Widdrington and owned by Mrs. Fox). Both were sired by the same dog, Sing Hi of Lhakang, bred by Mrs. Widdrington: Ch. Peregrin out of a gold bitch Golden Bobbin of Elfann (bred by Mrs. K. Mitchell) and Ch. Jen Kai Ko out of the black and white bitch Jessame of Lhakang (bred by Miss M. I. McMullen). One was strong in gold and the other in black and white, Ch. Jen Kai Ko coming through the Lunghwa line which is said to be strong in a good black, and Ch. Golden Peregrin from the golden line of Bobbin. Both have now sired champion stock, and each has the Swedish line of Jungfältets Jung Ming which carries both black/white and gold colourings. The line of Bobbin figures in many overseas golden champion pedigrees from Elfann stock.

Jungfältets Jung Ming (d). A Swedish import, and a great deal more influential than has ever been acknowledged. This line has its faults, and needs using selectively, but it also strongly counteracts faults in the Peke line. From mating to the bitch Tara of Clystvale, free of the Peke line, two dogs survived. One was Ch. Chi Ma Che of Antarctica (bred by Mrs. Longden) who in turn sired two champions, Ch. Chan Shih of Darite, and Ch. Kuang Kuang of Antarctica (both bred by Mr. and Mrs. Rawlings). This line followed through to Ch. Dominic of Telota (bred by Mrs. Newson) and Chs. Chaski and Che-Ko of Antarctica (bred by Mr. and Mrs. Rawlings).

The other surviving dog from the litter of four was my Snaefells Huckleberry Finn, who sired Ch. Dott of Gorseycop (bred by Mrs. Bennett, owned by Mrs. Hoare) and is grandsire to Ch. Newroots Nankipoo of Snaefell and many other excellent animals. As the owner, I am well aware of the points thrown by this Swedish line, which are as follows: good action and shoulders, level backs (progeny invariably develop evenly front and back), nice dark eyes, improvement of mouths and teeth but an inclination to the straight nose and lack of under-chin. Lightness of bone and height of leg both need watching. There is a shortage of hair on the legs in some specimens, but this improves with the second coat. A tight tail is thrown recessively, with varying degrees of tightness. Colours thrown are black/white, pastel shades and golds.

The survival of both Chi Ma Che and Huckleberry Finn was due to hand rearing by Miss Clark from the age of one week. The two remaining puppies in the litter, who remained with the dam and breeder, became ill and unfortunately died.

Mrs. Fowler of Chasmu was one of the earliest breeders, whose kennel was established in 1938. Having no progeny from her early gold and white specimens imported from China, she was determined to establish a gold line. Since this was the first attempt at any specific colour breeding, I feel it is of historical interest to the breed to give an account.

The foundation dog was gold/white Sui Yan – grandson of the Queen's imported Swedish Choo Choo who, although registered as black/white, did in fact have some brown on him in the early days. Sui Yan was bred to the chocolate and white bitch Madam Ko of Taishan (grand-daughter of the brown/white Canadian imported Tashi of Chouette), and the ensuing litter included two bitches: liver/white Ta Chi of Taishan (later the first champion of the breed) and gold/white Yi who became the foundation bitch of the Chasmu strain.

Yi was mated to Ch. Choo Ling, the only offspring being a white and brindle bitch called Om Mani Pudni. When she was bred back to her white/gold grandsire, Sui Yan, this mating produced many solid honey and honey/white colours with good black pigmentation, amongst which was the dog Ki Ming. Om Mani Pudni was then mated to the black Shebo Schunde of Hungjao, of the solid-coloured Ishuh Tzu line; there were some honey-coloured specimens, but in those where the gold had darkened it also blended with the black, therefore most of the puppies were a solid dark gold/brindle and one was a solid black (kepong). In 1954 one of this litter, a white/honey bitch, Golden Salween, was mated to her half-brother, Ki Ming, and produced the desired beautiful clear gold in a dog Tasmin, who on being mated to an equally clear gold bitch, Lhakang Mimosa of Northallerton, established this colour which is still with the kennel today. At the time of writing there are no English Champions of the solid gold colour, but two International Champions of this line – one owned by the late Comtesse d'Anjou

and the other by Mrs. Backx-Benninck. The breeding is sufficient
to show that this gold is a recessive colour.

Golden Tasmin (clear gold)	Ki Ming (w/honey)	Sui Yan (w/gold)
		Om Mani Pudni (w/brindle)
	Golden Salween (w/honey)	Shebo Schunde of Hungjao (black)
		Om Mani Pudni (w/brindle)
Lhakang Mimosa of Northallerton (clear gold)	Leo Lao of Lhakang (gold)	Shebo Tsemo of Lhakang (red/br/ white turned grey)
		Me of Lhakang (gold/white)
	Lotze of Lhakang (gold/white)	Wu Cheng of Lhakang (black/white) brother and sister Mao Wong of Lhakang (black/white)

General colour breeding will take some clarification, for every
new line has brought in a different colour, and fading genes to
add to the range. Personally, I rather hope that colouring will
never be too rigidly classified, since it is the diversity of colour
changes which makes the Shih Tzu so beautiful and interesting.
However, it is true that colour is becoming an increasingly
important factor as competition in the show ring becomes stiffer.

Markings of the Shih Tzu will in my opinion take precedence
over colour, for there are definite markings – in addition to the
highly prized white top-knot and tail tip on the parti-coloured –
which can certainly be specifically bred for. Examples are the large
white shawl, the saddle marking and the tiger stripes. I feel that
colour and markings should never take first place in the breeding,
for too much emphasis in this respect could mean that other
more important points are liable to suffer.

In concluding the chapter on lines and families, I would like to emphasise that it is not only the champion lines which are of prime importance in the breed; there are so many good dogs I would have liked to mention, who well deserve their championship, and a pedigree full of champions will not automatically guarantee a good dog.

4

The Standard

THE first standard of the breed was drawn up in 1935 by the Shih Tzu Club, under the guidance of General Sir Douglas and Lady Brownrigg and with the help of Mr. Croxton Smith, an important member of the Kennel Club; it was approved by Miss Hutchins, who had imported her dogs at the same time as the Brownriggs. This standard was then submitted to and approved by the Kennel Club as the breed's approved standard.

The Kauffmanns in Norway, who had imported their dogs at about the same time, had been in correspondence with the Brownriggs and, having compared notes and photographs, were agreed about the main points.

The standard was then considered to be 'suitable for a beginning', the idea being that it should be fairly loose in concept in order to allow scope for improvement within the breed. At that time there was a total of forty-three registrations.

Although the breed had been in this country for fifteen years, and was much more firmly established, a severe setback had necessarily occurred during the war years. A new standard was drawn up in 1948:

BREED STANDARD 1948

Head Broad, round, wide between the eyes; shock-headed with hair falling over the eyes; good beard and whiskers, the hair growing upwards on the nose giving a distinctly chrysanthemum-like effect.

Eyes Large, dark and round. (By 1949 it was considered necessary to include 'but not prominent'.)

Muzzle Square, short, but not wrinkled like a Pekingese, flat and hairy.

Ears Large, and carried drooping, so heavily coated that they appear to blend with the hair of the neck.

Body Body between withers and root of tail should be considerably longer than the height of withers, well ribbed up.

Legs Short, straight and muscular, heavily coated, with feet big and hair between pads. (Notice the word 'straight', which was in the standard from the beginning, and was always aimed for. In 1953 the word 'straight' was deleted from the standard, since it was realised that the leg bones were not straight when compared with those, for example, of a terrier. As this alteration followed on the Peke cross, it is natural that people assumed it was removed in order to permit a bow which might have been introduced by the cross. Unfortunately, nothing replaced 'straight' to show that the bow was not permitted, although it is an understood point. There were some bad fronts prior to the cross, but this was not considered to be correct, hence the insertion of 'straight' in the original standard.)

Tail Heavily coated and curled well over back, set on high.

Coat Long and dense but not curly; looks harsher than it feels to the touch.

Colours All colours, but a white blaze on the forehead and a white tip to the tail are highly prized.

Size About 11 in at the withers, but considerable variation from this standard is permissible, provided other proportions are correct and true to type. (It was recognised by those who had seen the dogs in China that there was a great variation in size, and it was considered more important to get the dog firmly established and to conform to the standard, than to throw out good specimens on grounds of size alone.)

General Appearance Not toys, very active, lively and alert, with a distinctly arrogant carriage.

   In some ways breeding to type in the early pioneer days must have been easier, since the sole aim of those concerned was to improve the breed, and this was watched over with a careful eye by Lady Brownrigg who, as has been previously stated, travelled round inspecting as many of the puppies as possible. If she could not see them, then letters were sent giving minute details. Whenever possible, puppies were placed with people who would breed or show, and faulty dogs were sold cheaply as pets. Sometimes points which are not nowadays regarded as faults were then considered undesirable, and however good the animal was otherwise it would then be sold as a pet. One example of this was to show the white cornea of the eye, which was referred to as a squint: it was not considered good to show any white.

The main objective was to keep the breed to the original size, a medium 12–14 lb in weight. Lady Brownrigg had after all selected her dogs with considerable care, refusing to buy any larger or smaller ones which were offered to her.

Each fresh import has brought in good and bad traits, and each year sees different points change for better or worse. It is the breeder's responsibility to recognise this, and not to be 'kennel blind', for a dog is usually judged as a whole and not on individual points; in this way a bad feature can very easily sweep imperceptibly through a breed, carried by a prolific champion stud dog. The only way to prevent this from happening is to know the standard thoroughly and to be able to recognise both good and bad in one's own dogs – should you think your dog is perfect, remember that it may be only in your eyes that it is so!

The unwritten part of a standard, or the implications lying behind it, are as important as the features which are actually written into it.

Here follows today's standard, reproduced by kind permission of the Kennel Club:

CURRENT BREED STANDARD

General Appearance Very active, lively and alert, with a distinctly arrogant carriage. The Shih Tzu is neither a terrier nor a toy dog.

Head and Skull Head broad and round, wide between the eyes. Shock-headed with hair falling well over the eyes. Good beard and whiskers; the hair growing upwards on the nose gives a distinctly chrysanthemum-like effect. Muzzle square and short, but not wrinkled like a Pekingese; flat and hairy. Nose black for preference and about one inch from tip to stop.

Eyes Large, dark and round but not prominent.

Ears Large, with long leathers, and carried drooping. Set slightly below the crown of the skull; so heavily coated that they appear to blend with the hair of the neck.

Mouth Level or slightly underhung.

Forequarters Legs short and muscular with ample bone. The legs should look massive on account of the wealth of hair.

Body Body between withers and root of tail should be longer than height at withers; well-coupled and sturdy; chest broad and deep, shoulders firm, back level.

Hindquarters Legs short and muscular with ample bone. They should look straight when viewed from the rear. Thighs well-rounded and muscular. Legs should look massive on account of the wealth of the hair.

Feet Firm and well-padded. They should look big on account of the wealth of hair.

Tail Heavily plumed, curled well over back; carried gaily, set on high.

Coat Long and dense, but not curly, with good undercoat.

Colour All colours permissible, but a white blaze on the forehead and a white tip to the tail are highly prized. Dogs with liver markings have dark liver noses and slightly lighter eyes. Pigmentation on muzzle as unbroken as possible.

Weight and Size 10–18 lb, ideal weight 9–16 lb. Height at withers, not more than 10½ in. Type and breed characteristics of the greatest importance and on no account to be sacrificed to size alone.

Faults Narrow heads, pig jaws, snipeyness, pale-pink noses and eye-rims, small or light eyes, legginess, sparse coat.

Clarification of the standard

General Appearance This is self-explanatory, for alertness should be seen in the show ring, and the Shih Tzu should be quick and ready to move.

Conformation in the show ring can be seen as both stationary and functional. A dog which is only good when 'set up' is not of good intrinsic merit. It should also be good on the move, and if the conformation is incorrect this cannot be so. The standing position should be adopted naturally, and the animal should be capable of holding its tail well curled over the back. Where puppies are concerned it is excusable to help to position them, for they are learning, and may find the atmosphere of the ring unnerving.

Head, Mouth and Skull The size of the head should be in balance with the body, and – together with the neck – in balance with the tail. Hence the saying 'you can't tell which end is which'.

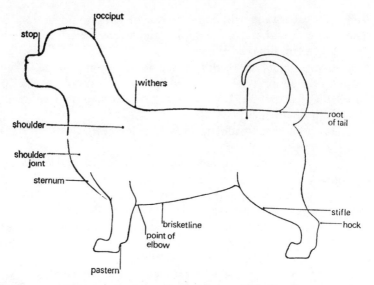

Figure 1 Body outline with anatomical points

A well-dressed head can do much to improve a dog's appearance. Height and breadth can be altered with good furnishings, and the length of nose and width between the eyes can appear

Figure 2 The Head

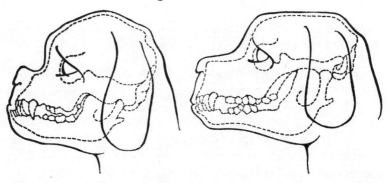

(a) correct skull; good stop; slightly uptilted nose; proportions approximately from nose to stop and stop to occiput as 1 is to 4 or 5

(b) incorrect skull; nose long and turned downwards; stop too shallow

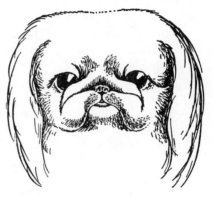

(d) head of Pekingese for comparison; flat skull, large prominent eyes; ears set high on skull

(c) correct head; ears set on below the crown; round eyes, large but not prominent; top of nose level with bottom of eyes

(e) head of Lhasa Apso for comparison; narrower head; nose a little lower and longer

different according to how the top-knot is tied. It is essential to examine the head closely from all angles, for a ringside view or a photograph can be very deceptive. A good head is of the utmost importance, and should resemble neither the Apso nor the Pekingese.

The nose, which is ideally about an inch from tip to stop, should spring from a deep stop on a level with or immediately below the eye rims; it may be level or tilted slightly upwards – a downward nose gives the wrong expression, while an uptilted nose imparts a more arrogant aspect. The smaller dog should have a proportionately smaller nose. Lack of chin is sometimes seen with the straight nose, and too strong an under-jaw with the uptilted type.

Wide nostrils are preferred, for tight nostrils in whelps can cause trouble.

The eyes should not be so large that they seem disproportionate to the head, and it is preferable that they show no white, although this feature is rather strongly in the breed at the present time and an otherwise good dog is seldom penalised for it. However, it should be recognised that it *is* undesirable, and not bred in.

Mouth Wry and over-shot jaws are faults; the jaw should be square to give the Chinese lion-like appearance. Although the bite

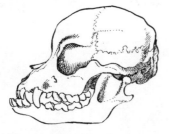   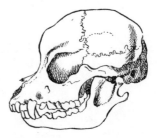

(a) correct; undershot ⅛ inch   (b) incorrect; overshot
or level

(c) correct square jaw

Figure 3 The Bite

is level or undershot, the upper lips should come over the lower when the mouth is closed, and the teeth should not show.

Teeth There should be six incisors in each jaw; these are the front teeth between the canines. Many dogs have only four, which I think is common to brachycephalic or short-faced dogs. Fewer than four incisors is definitely undesirable, for too few teeth will give a narrow jaw.

Judges are still lenient over teeth in England, though not necessarily in other countries. However, it is noticeable that some kennels are working to improve this point.

The measurements of the head are about 4–1 of the nose length from the stop to the occiput of the skull. The head of the male is larger than that of the female, and should appear more masculine. The bitch has a definitely feminine expression, and it is usually possible for a knowledgeable person to tell the difference between the sexes at a glance. Pastel-shaded dogs should not be referred to as 'bitchy' purely on grounds of colour.

Forequarters These must take in the neck, set-on of head and shoulder placement, for each is relative to the other.

This part of the written standard is, in my opinion, inadequate. The set-on of the head and placement of the scapula are most important. There have been many arguments over the length of neck; some people maintain that it should be short, and fear that a long neck will give a long back, but the geneticists say that this is not so and that although the bones of the thoracic and cervical vertebrae go together, the various parts of the spine have their own genes. In cases where both the cervical and thoracic bones are short, the front action is unlikely to be very free, and the dog will be either short in length or too long in loin.

For correct front action and set-on of the head, the shoulders should be 'laid back' and the cervical bones long, giving a long chest. As the scapula is attached at an inclined angle, more cervical or neck bones show. If the shoulder is upright it will cover the lower cervical vertebrae, giving the impression that the neck is short, and that the head is attached at a perpendicular angle instead of gently sloping as it should. The attachment of the scapular muscles is also relative to the importance of the action, a good forequarter being essential for the right front action in which so many dogs fail – this failure being easily disguised by a full coat and expert handling.

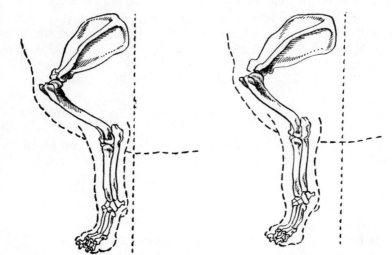

(a) correct; line through withers   (b) incorrect; humerus too short;
    to foot perpendicular   elbow too far forward

Figure 4 Forequarters

To come to the leg, the standard says 'short', but the question is, how short? This is where the danger lies; it is common in breeding to exaggerate specified points when there is no maximum or minimum measurement. In the past, if a dog's legs were too short, Lady Brownrigg would say it was 'a walking caterpillar'!

So far as balance is concerned, the dog should be longer from *withers* to root of tail than its height at the withers, not from the point of the shoulder as in the Apso. The elbows are ideally level with or very slightly above the brisket line, the elbow joint coming directly under the withers with the foot directly under that. The distance from elbow to withers is a little greater than that from elbow to ground. In fact, it should be possible to draw a perpendicular line from the withers to the foot. The scapula and upper and lower bones of the leg should be approximately equal in length; if the humerus is short the action is sure to be affected,

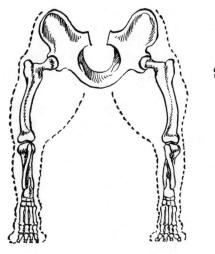

(a) correct; legs straight

(b) incorrect; cowhocked

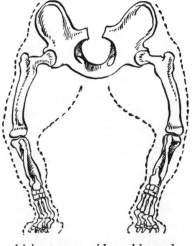

(c) incorrect; wide and bowed

Figure 5 Hindquarters from rear

since the elbow will be too far forward; this will make the dog down in front unless accompanied by a too upright shoulder. The legs should appear massive on account of the wealth of hair, the bone itself being ample rather than massive; the legs should not be bowed. The feet should point straight ahead, which they seldom do if there is any bowing, although this discrepancy is frequently concealed by the long coat coupled with 'stringing'* the dog.

Body As has been stated, the length of the body from withers to the root of the tail should be greater than the height at the withers. The body should be short coupled, which is very different from being 'cobby' or short in length – how often one hears the comment 'he is so nice and short', which is inaccurate as is clearly explained in *The Dog in Action* (p. 32), i.e. 'the coupling is the distance between the front assembly and the back assembly'. It is not desirable for a Shih Tzu to be too long cast, for this has been known to give rise to disc trouble. On the other hand, too short a back will not permit the typical action.

Chest This should be broad and deep, not barrel as it is in some cases inaccurately described. Too much barrel will give the undesirable Pekingese front roll.

The body of the Shih Tzu does not have a waist, neither should it be 'tucked-up' nor tapered behind. The underline should remain nearly parallel to the upper line.

The body should be muscular rather than fat, and in hard condition; it should be possible to feel the ribs. The breed originated in Tibet as an active dog even if it led a more pampered life in the Imperial Palace of China.

The top line should be level, which means there should be no roach, nor up behind. The latter is frequently disguised by the tail when stationary conformation is being judged. This is a feature which has been in the dogs from the earliest imports, not in the line from Hibou but certainly in Shu Ssa's line; more-over, it was permitted in the Chinese standard. There are varying degrees of being up behind, and, whereas this can occur in very slight degree and may be a small point compared with others, when more pronounced it is usually accompanied by other faults such as straight stifle or incorrect forequarters.

---

* Walking the dog on a tightly drawn lead. In this way extra support is given to the muscles of the forequarter.

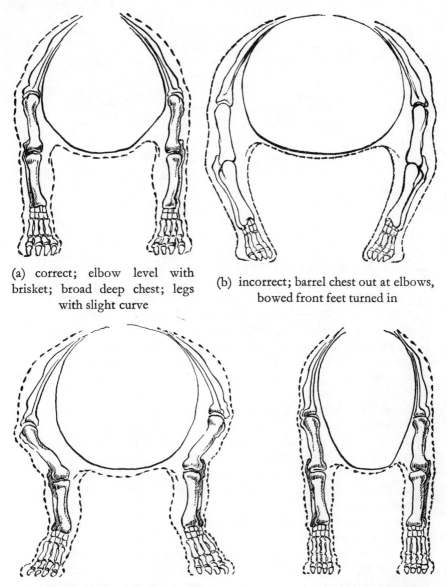

(a) correct; elbow level with brisket; broad deep chest; legs with slight curve

(b) incorrect; barrel chest out at elbows, bowed front feet turned in

(c) incorrect 'Peke-type'; 'Queen Anne' legs; toes turned out

(d) incorrect 'Terrier-type'; front too narrow; legs too straight

Figure 6 Fronts

(a) correct; level

(b) incorrect; high in hindquarters

(c) incorrect; roached

Figure 7 Toplines

Feet At one time it was stated that there should be hair between the pads; this is no longer in the standard, and in fact hair is now frequently cut out in order to prevent matting and discomfort to the dogs. The pads themselves should be thick.

Hindquarters It is important to have some bend of stifle, since too straight a stifle will give a stilted action. The legs should appear straight from behind, and the feet should turn neither in nor out. There should be no 'cowhocks' and no bowing.

Tail This should be set on high, should balance the head and be well feathered. It should not be brought over and laid flat on the back, but should be a 'teapot handle' tail with the feathering falling to the side of the dog. A tight tail is incorrect, and although this is a point which can be easily bred out, and is in no way detrimental to the well-being of the animal, it is nevertheless heavily penalised in the show ring when it spoils the balanced picture of the dog.

Coat The texture of the coat is not described in the standard, but the nearest comparison is to liken it to human hair. It varies in texture with different colours, and indeed it is possible to find black and white hairs alternating on one strand, each of a different texture such that the difference can be felt as one passes it through the fingers. The coat should be neither dead straight nor silky; a slight wave is permitted, but not a curl, and a natural parting should form down the back. A long flowing coat is to be desired, but one trailing on the ground is quite unsuitable in this

(a) correct; pot-handle tail (over back hanging to one side)

(b) incorrect; low set

(c) incorrect; flat to back

(d) incorrect; skew too tight

Figure 8 Tail set

Figure 9 Relationship of coat to dog underneath

active breed. Lady Brownrigg liked to 'see daylight' under the
dog. Over-emphasis on the coat is liable to lead to neglect of
other more important points in overall structure and soundness.
Colour All colours are permissible; the solid lion gold dog
usually has a black mask and ear fringes. Gold and yellows were
the favoured colours of the Chinese, and gold shades predominate
at the present time, black and white now being quite scarce. In a
gold class one can see dogs ranging in colour from silver – with
one gold streak – to brilliant apricot, and even true liver with the
liver nose. Although the gold class makes a spectacular show for
the ringsider, it is disappointing to judge, since most dogs have
already been previously placed, and although this is a colour class
it may not take precedence over quality. Understandably, therefore, there is frequently discontent amongst the exhibitors!
Weight and Size This is the most disputed part of the standard.
Firstly, the Shih Tzu is inclined to be heavy for its size, and weight
comparisons are not therefore very significant. Also, a dog
becomes heavier with advancing years, thus a young adult of
18 lb may well reach 23 lb with age.

There has always been a considerable variation in the size of
the Shih Tzu, and this has been generally accepted. According to
many authorities, there were both small and large dogs in China
and Tibet. All sizes within the standard of 10–18 lb and up to
$10\frac{1}{2}$ in in height are permissible. It is more difficult to breed a good
small dog than a good large specimen, since proportions must be
more exact when the size is small. Also, a small dog must be
quite solid and not just the smallest dog in a litter. There is need
for all sizes; it should always be remembered that weight and
size are relative to each other, and that the standard lays down that
'type and breed characteristics are of the greatest importance and
on no account to be sacrificed to size alone'.
Faults These are listed clearly, although I hope the time will
come when the lighter eye is permitted in certain of the grey
shades, especially in the blue-grey, as well as in livers, for we do
have that colour.
Action This is one of the most important aspects of the Shih
Tzu, as indeed of every breed. As one observer is reputed to have
said to another at the ringside, on seeing an unsound dog placed
first, 'How do you like that?' 'Well,' said the second, 'he has a
beautiful head.' 'He can't walk on his —— head,' said the first!

In a beauty contest, a beautiful girl would not be expected to win if she were only capable of looking beautiful when placed in a standing position – the judges would look ridiculous if she went off walking with a limp after they had awarded her the crown! However, I am afraid that this can happen with dogs; the dog must not only be typical of its breed but also sound in action. The true Shih Tzu action is a great joy to watch; with their lovely flowing coats and free movement, they are frequently likened to a ship in full sail or a hovercraft, for 'they float as if on a cloud'.

The ideal action should be free. In front the legs should go straight, the feet turning neither in nor out; the latter should not be swung forward like those of a terrier, neither should they walk as if slack in the pastern. The head should be held high, without the need to be 'strung up'.

In the hind action the legs should look straight; although 'flung out' behind to show the whole pad, they should be fairly close, but never so close that they brush against or go in a straight line with each other. A stilted hind action is quite incorrect; there should be no weaving, plaiting or padding, dragging of one leg or frequent hopping – the action must be clean and straight. A slight roll is permitted owing to the broad deep chest, and this can also occur when a dog walks too fast – for a split second all four legs are off the ground and the animal comes down into a roll (this can best be seen in slow motion).

Generally, the dog should walk gaily with its head and tail held high. Shih Tzu should be capable of walking on a slack lead, and this is the only way that correct front action can be assessed. If the dog is not put together correctly it will not walk properly. Should the hindquarters be particularly good, and the forequarters only indifferent, he may not walk in the right way, and in this case it may in fact be better if both ends were mediocre. Each bone, joint and muscle is related to the other, and synchronisation between front and rear is all-important.

It should be appreciated that a standard is only a guide line, since no dogs are absolutely perfect, and interpretations of a standard always vary. It would be quite impossible to include minute details and expect nature to conform, therefore there will always be some variety of type, and of course people also vary considerably in their preference for one feature or another. This is why individual strains differ, so it is sensible to decide on what one considers to be ideal within the standard, and to breed to this. It is well known that some people are liable to interpret a standard to the likeness of the breed of dogs they have previously owned, and while I do not feel this can really apply where breeds are totally different, nevertheless it can happen where similar breeds are involved and is very much to be deprecated. Another failing is to identify perfection with one's first and often best-loved Shih Tzu, blinding oneself to its faults and – rightly or wrongly – breeding to this type; this is kennel blindness.

5
Character and Training

Character

This chapter on the Shih Tzu character should really be read in conjunction with the chapters on breeding, for it is not sufficient to breed for looks alone. Although the dog can be a delightful object of beauty when seen poised in the show ring, with its long flowing coat and superbly groomed, it doesn't stay that way for long! After a few mad turns rushing round the garden or park, or on the lawn in a heavy dew, sweeping up the garden leaves as though it were a garden broom, you realise that it is the character of the dog which really matters. The big question in judging is 'which comes first, soundness or type?'; but to the breeder, soundness, type and character should all be of equal importance.

One needs to distinguish between inherited character and environmental character, also to take account of family characteristics with the breed. Here I quoted from Clarence Pfaffenberger's *Dog Behavior:* 'Environment has never made a man, animal or plant any better than the genes he or it inherited. What is often referred to as an ideal "climate" can help any individual achieve his potential or nearly his potential. Poor environment can cripple the development of an individual until he can never achieve the potential he was born with, even if an ideal climate is later provided.' To those readers who are perhaps reading this book in an effort to make up their minds whether or not this is the breed for them, I will do my best to describe this fascinating little dog, who – partly for his changing mood – has been referred to poetically by some as 'the fairy dog'.

In the past, in Tibet, the Shih Tzu was always kept as a member of the family and a holy dog who could do no wrong. He lived with the family, and became very humanised. In China, in the Imperial Palace, he was treated as a great pet with his own eunuchs to look after him, and here he was taught a great deal. This past history of the Shih Tzu has obviously played a large

part in its character formation. He can learn without being taught
so long as he is given some idea of what is expected of him; he
loves to demonstrate his accomplishments in this respect, and
has often learned to retrieve with labradors merely by observing
and copying them.

Members of this breed need to be brought up as a child of the
family, and if there is a child for company, so much the better.
The child should learn to have as much respect for the dog as the
dog is expected to have for the child; it is cruel to allow a small
baby to pull and poke a dog around, and even if the dog does put
up with it this is no excuse!

The Shih Tzu is capable of giving utter devotion and hours of
fun and amusement, but he is not 'your servant the dog' and
will expect you to respond in return; like many other dogs, he
thinks he is your equal if not your superior! If he does not get
plenty of human companionship he is quite incapable of developing his full character, and whereas this could be applied to many
breeds the Shih Tzu has a considerably greater potential than
some.

It is very difficult to give an adequate description of the Shih
Tzu's character, for one really needs to be an owner in order to
appreciate it fully. As James Mumfor wrote in a delightful article
in the American *Shih Tzu News*:

No-one knows how they (the eunuchs) added a dash of lion, several
teaspoons of rabbit, a couple of ounces of domestic cat, one part
court jester, a dash of ballerina, a pinch of old man (Chinese), a bit of
beggar, a tablespoon of monkey, one part baby seal, a dash of teddy
bear, and the rest, dogs of Tibetan and Chinese origin.

This gives a wonderful picture of the Shih Tzu – its character
is so very versatile!

There are very definite family characteristics which can be
recognised, and it is only by owning various blood lines, and
several generations of the same family, that you identify these
traits. Shih Tzu do not breed like peas out of a pod, all identical.
This is a happy little dog, full of fun, and seldom belligerent;
he usually gets on well with other breeds, except when as one of a
group he reverts to the natural mobbing instinct. Should a visiting
dog arrive at the house, the Shih Tzu can be relied upon to meet it

Ch. Shebo Tsemo of Lhakang

Ch. Wang Poo of Taishan

Puppy at ten days

At six weeks

(Alison Snell)

At nine weeks

(Diane Pearce)

Fully grown – at twelve months

Three champions from the same litter. Zeus of Bridgend, Sue Lin of Bridgend, and Tricina Wen Mo of Bridgend

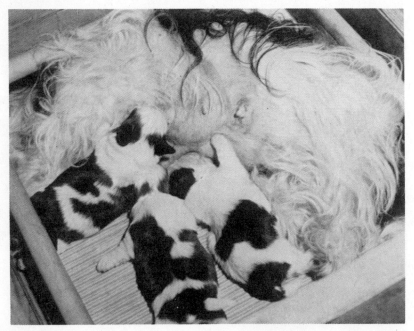

(Alison Snell)

Flat puppy in the nest. It was standing and walking normally at six weeks

with courtesy, albeit treating human visitors with dignified aloofness, though some lines are much more friendly to strangers than others. He will not accept someone into the house without your approval!

Wilfulness and disobedience are faults of which he is accused. Wilful he is, but I cannot help wondering whether any disobedience could be the fault of those responsible for training him. Training *must* begin very early in his life, and to call him to 'come' at five weeks is not too soon.

As was stressed earlier, one of the great assets of the breed is its ease in whelping. A Shih Tzu bitch is usually an excellent mother, giving complete and untiring devotion to her puppies long after weaning. Their hearing is very keen, particularly when they are alert with a litter, and they are very sensitive to anything unusual going on either indoors or outside. They also have an acute awareness of atmosphere, and are extremely observant.

If you pick up a Shih Tzu in your arms it will lie quite still, and even the puppies seldom wriggle. When put down, however, it comes to life, rushing round and round at top speed, dodging obstacles, chasing in and out, up and down, missing nothing, knocking nothing, until it finally drops exhausted – only to rise again and repeat the performance! Pastmasters at the game of tag,

Figure 10 Shih Tzu often lie with their hind legs extended

Shih Tzu are rightly labelled 'clowns of the dog world'! To watch them at play can give endless enjoyment and amusement. It is not only sad but unnecessary when a dog is kept on its own and never allowed to play, just in order to preserve its coat for showing.

The Shih Tzu has a fascinating way of lying flat on the ground with legs outstretched; he will also sit patiently waiting, remaining so still that he looks like a small Buddha, his eyes gazing intently on your face, waiting for your next move; you can be sure he'll be beside you when you make it! Visitors are always impressed when they see six or more of my dogs in the room, all sitting motionless with expressive eyes gazing up at me. There is one exception, however: Eliza Doolittle, who always sets her gaze (and herself if possible) on the visitor!

I said earlier in this chapter that the Shih Tzu is not naturally belligerent, but if attacked he will stand his ground, and usually comes off worst which can often be the cause of losing an eye. It is not in the nature of the breed to lose face, so he should not run away. A second dog will always go to the aid of a friend, and will rush in and out biting the legs or any other accessible part of the assailant's anatomy. When this happens at home, particularly if one of them has 'told off' a puppy, another will fly to the rescue, then another will attack that one, and so on until they look remarkably like a rugby scrum. The trouble is that they forget who was the original troublemaker, and make it an excuse to have a good old free-for-all. The answer to this is to pick one up by the scruff of the neck to avoid getting bitten and remove it from the room, but you will find that instead of seizing just one, you have several others still hanging on to each other's tails. However, this sort of fighting is seldom serious.

Have you ever seen a dog smile? Shih Tzus do, and mine seem to do it mainly in anticipation of a tit-bit. The asparagus season brings them flocking to the table showing large expanses of teeth, and brussels sprouts are another great favourite. Of course, anything from our table tastes infinitely better than their own food!

This breed is very adaptable so long as it has been properly socialised, and will fit into both town and country environments, but must have human companionship. It is certainly not a dog it is advisable to leave if you have to be out at work all day.

Shih Tzus thoroughly enjoy a good country walk, and are quite capable of keeping up with most breeds; indeed, many of them go out exercising with horses. On the other hand, a flat in town with walks in the park is quite adequate, and your dog will be perfectly happy with this life so long as you are around. By being around, I do not mean that it cannot be left for reasonable periods of time. This, like so many things, is largely a matter of early training, and something to which they can be accustomed from puppy days. To take a dog out shopping is not much fun for dog or owner.

The Shih Tzu is generally a robust little dog, and if well cared for should not require much veterinary attention. Both sexes are very affectionate; the dog in this breed is quite as affectionate as the bitch, so do not be misled into thinking that you must have a bitch rather than a dog for this reason.

Many Shih Tzu love swimming, but I do feel this should not be encouraged, since they are apt to jump into any dirty old pond and come out stinking! There is also the risk that they may rush into a fast-flowing stream, and be liable to get swept away with the current. Some are climbers and some are diggers – few are both, and many are neither. Most will jump if taught to do so, and they all learn tricks very easily. They have a strange habit of sitting on your chair as soon as you get up, because they do not like to sit on the ground! If there is a table by a window on which they can climb, they will most likely think it was put there especially for their benefit, and there they will sit, looking like models in the window.

The character which I have tried to describe is obviously the general character of the breed; there are so many other fascinating little ways of behaviour which are peculiar either to an individual or a family within the breed: dancing on the hind legs, and welcoming you in this way by stretching out the front paws as it dances; welcoming you by picking up the hem of your garment (though mini-skirts have discouraged this trick) and bringing you presents. When quite overcome by excitement it will snort and snort and gurgle in its throat, or instead it will 'talk'. It has a fascinating habit of burying nothing, covering it with nothing, and then walking away contentedly! Or nosing up its food dish and hiding the food, although this is mostly observed with the brood bitch. It also has a special way of cleaning its face and

whiskers. I could go on and on indefinitely, but it is only by
owning a Shih Tzu and having it as a constant companion that you
can really get to know the breed.

Most Shih Tzu are quite content to stay around the home, but
occasionally you will find that you have a wanderer; this can be
of either sex, and it is most important that you teach it some
obedience, since the breed has little road sense. At least teach it
the command 'stay'.

Many people enquire whether these are sporty dogs. The answer
is 'yes', and if given the chance they will chase after chickens, so
they have to be trained not to do this. Neither should they be
turned into 'toy' or 'lap dogs', for this completely ruins their
characters.

Most of the Shih Tzu I know of and have met have wonderful
characters, and this is a great strength in the breed. I feel that
some breeders are not fully aware of the emotional upset which
can be caused by uprooting a dog from the home kennel, where it
has been perfectly happy, and transferring it to a new home at the
wrong age, without its first being fully socialised. Much research
is being devoted to the subject, and more knowledge in this
respect would enable us to keep our breed strong in the correct
character and temperament.

It is not surprising that the Buddhists classified the dog at the
top of the ladder next to humans, for they were considered to be
reincarnated humans who had erred during their lifetime. I only
wish that as high a proportion of the human race possessed the
same delightful characters as the Shih Tzu!

Training

To know the character of the breed is one great help towards
successful training. For one thing, this is a wilful and stubborn
breed. The Shih Tzu will be devoted to you so long as you treat
him as a member of your family, and that does not involve giving
him the same food but showing that you love and respect him.
Early and sufficient training is most important, so that he learns
to use his brain while young. Whether you have just bought a new
puppy at eight weeks old, or are a breeder running puppies on,
the procedure is basically the same.

According to Scott and Fuller in *Genetics and Social Behavior of the Dog,* a puppy's nervous system is developing between three and seven weeks of age, and by eight weeks it has the capacity if not the experience of an adult. Early attention from humans, as well as the companionship of other dogs (i.e. its litter mates), is most important. It is absolutely essential that puppies from three weeks of age should have love and attention from both the owner and the dog mother, if they are to end up really well adjusted. A puppy will transfer its affection straight away to a new owner, for what it needs and wants is love, regardless of who is giving it.

When you first take over the ownership of your new puppy, keep to the same diet and temperature conditions which were used in the home kennel. If the puppy has already been acclimatised to weather, and to sleeping in an unheated room, do not start to mollycoddle it. On the other hand, if it has not yet been outside (and this is difficult with winter puppies), care should be taken lest the nostrils tighten up and force it to breathe through its mouth. This tightening of the nostrils can happen very easily in a small puppy due to changes in temperature, so do be very careful not to transfer a pup from a heated atmosphere into the cold, or to allow him to stay outside longer than is absolutely necessary. Too much heat can be equally harmful.

For the first few nights the puppy is bound to miss his companions, for he will have been accustomed to snuggling up to them (and probably his mother as well) for warmth. If you replace this warmth with a *warm*, not hot, bottle, wrapped in some woolly material, he will usually settle down very quickly. Leave some newspapers on the floor in case he wakes before you go into him in the morning, but at this stage it is better for you to get up early and take him straight out to relieve himself, telling him how good he is when he has obliged. Always remember the word of praise, and make this exaggerated, also the word of disapproval. Above all, be consistent, and do not permit one day something for which you admonish him the next. Try always to keep to a strictly routine timetable, especially with feeding.

A puppy, like a baby, needs plenty of undisturbed rest. He usually likes to sleep after a meal, so make a point of shutting him away from possible disturbances so that he can do so in peace.

Holding the puppy

Do not make a practice of lifting a dog by the scruff of the neck, for there is far too much weight in the body, particularly as the dog gets older. Do not hold him by putting your hand under the elbows, against the side of the chest, for this is likely to push the elbows out and completely spoil the animal's front; even if you do not intend to show him, you want him to grow up correctly. Pick him up with the palm of your hand under the brisket, or under the tummy and chest, with your finger and thumb *outside* each elbow; then, as the puppy grows, your full hand will take the brisket. Your left hand should support the body by placing it under the tail and hindquarters.

Most Shih Tzu love to be picked up and cuddled, and will lie still for hours, but with an unfamiliar child a puppy may wriggle and try to jump down, so if there is a small child holding the puppy, let them both be near the ground, then puppy and child can get used to each other in safety. If a puppy jumps from a height it may injure itself.

Beds

The puppy should be given a bed of his own, off the ground and out of draughts. If he has a wicker basket, see that he does not chew it, and leave jagged ends, for these are dangerous to the eyes and can also catch in an adult's coat. Bind round any jagged ends for safety.

Basic commands, collar and lead training

I consider that basic training should have been accomplished before the puppy is eight weeks old, so that he can learn his name and respond to the command 'come' as soon as he is on his feet. Recognising the breeder through this response can vary within the litter by as much as one to two weeks. Once taught, training must be continued; sound obedience training has averted many a catastrophe.

If your puppy has not yet been taught to 'come', then don't waste time but begin to train him *now*. Once a name has already been given, and he has learned to respond to it, do not change this suddenly and completely even if you do not want him to keep it permanently. It is far better to continue using the original name, adding any new name after it; for example, if it has been called Fu and you want to rename it Ming, start with Fu Ming and then you can gradually drop the first part.

Each time the puppy comes to your call, make a great fuss of him, and sometimes give him a tit-bit. First of all, he must learn that it is fun to come to you, then this will become a habit. When he comes, get him to follow you by calling his name, playing with him, clapping your hands and so on, anything to hold his interest and attract him to come after you.

The next step is putting on a collar, preferably a soft one at first and for gradually increasing periods. I use a cat collar. If you have bought a harness, get rid of it – it will only make him 'out at shoulder'. When he is accustomed to the collar – and he may scratch at first – attach a piece of string or a light nylon lead, but leave this dangling at first so that he gets used to the feel of it. Next, pick up the end of the lead and let the puppy lead you, which he will love to do. Never pull or force him, he must become accustomed to things at his own pace, and will do so quite quickly. The next stage is to lead him for a little way, then if he pulls let him lead you again, calling him along in the same way as when you have been training him to come; lead him further, and gradually he will let you do the leading all the time. The time this will take obviously varies, most Shih Tzu are very easy to lead-train. Six weeks is really the best age to start, and it is ideal to undertake lead-training in a quiet area away from distractions.

By the age of twelve weeks the puppy will start to explore further away from the home; there will now be many more distractions, and a little more bribery may be required.

If you have a large garden, it is unwise to allow the young puppy to have the full run of it, for this is inviting trouble. Left to his own devices, he will gradually explore a little further each day, and will find everything very exciting. It is much wiser to wire off part of the garden. Never leave him sitting in the full sun, ensure that you give him shade as well, and provide water for him to drink. Give him some toys to play with, or he will dig holes in your lawn if he gets bored with nothing to do!

Inoculation

Although this is not strictly part of training, the latter cannot be
completed until after the puppy has gained some immunity.
Once inoculation is over, however, he can be taken out and
about to see the world and to become used to traffic. If he
appears frightened, soothe him, and make these excursions short
at first. It is important that he should become familiar with as
many as possible of the things which he will encounter during his
lifetime. An animal is far more likely to be shy if he has not been
able to get about and meet people before the age of sixteen weeks.
Between twelve and twenty-six weeks is another critical period,
when it is best not to let the puppy become too familiar with only
one place and one person. This applies not only to a Shih Tzu but
to all breeds. The experts consider that socialisation and localisa-
tion are interrelated, which is definitely true of the Shih Tzu, for
they are exceptionally sensitive to different surroundings and
new things.

Do not take your puppy for long walks at this age, six months
is quite early enough for this. Short walks on the lead to help
tighten up his muscles, combined with free play in the garden,
will give him all the exercise he needs now.

The car

Accustom the puppy to the car at an early age. This should prevent
any tendency to car sickness, which is frequently associated with
fear (see also Ailments section).

Obedience

A word which your puppy *must* learn right from the start is 'No',
and this should be said in a very firm authoritative tone, so that
he realises immediately that you disapprove. There is no need for
smacking, which is far more likely to make a dog disobedient.
Why should he want to come to a person who inflicts pain?
Exaggerate the tones in your voice for both approval and disapproval; it is the actual tone to which the dog responds.

Biting

Many young puppies will bite in play or in their excitement at welcoming you, but they must be taught that this is wrong before they are sixteen weeks old, for this is the age at which they learn who is the master, and a Shih Tzu will not be slow to decide that *he* is the master. If you have a real 'he-man' dog who does not like to be cuddled, respect this in him but on no account allow him to have his own way through growling; if you do, it could lead to biting. Admonish him severely, and go ahead with what you intended to do. Should he ever think you are frightened of him, his quick and intelligent brain will soon know that this is how he can get his own way. If he seems of uncertain temperament, I would suggest you consult your veterinarian, for a cryptorchid – for example – can behave in this way due to a hormone imbalance. The normal character of the Shih Tzu is not bad-tempered, for it is quite contrary to the breed, but it can be caused through mismanagement and is sometimes due to excessive and unrestrained teasing and harassment from small children. There are people who buy a puppy as a live toy for their children; they train neither the puppy nor their children, and both turn nasty. It is, of course, the puppy who is blamed for this state of affairs. There is no better pet for a child than a Shih Tzu, but as a companion and not a toy. Given the right guidance, children are wonderful at training dogs, and they love to feel that they have something of their very own who loves them and behaves better for them than for anybody else.

House training

A puppy is naturally clean, and as soon as it is able to crawl from the nest it will do so in order to relieve itself. This is the age to train it to use newspaper, which is a great help with a winter puppy, though I prefer to train a summer puppy straight away to go in the garden. This may mean more puddles in the house at first, but training is quicker in the end. If you begin by training on newspaper, this is useful, but must be followed by further training out of doors. Any puddles on the carpet should be wiped up immediately, and if soda water is squirted on the spot this will neutralise the urine. I knew one owner who had such difficulty

F

in training his puppy off the newspaper that he had to trail a piece after the puppy in a London street!

If the puppy is put out directly he wakes up, wait for him outside and tell him to spend his penny (or whatever phrase you prefer), but *always use the same word*. Then praise him well, he must associate the action with the word. A puppy can last for many hours at night, but will do numerous thimblefuls during the day, and at first you will not be able to put him out each time. Therefore choose your times, for example always after he has slept, after a meal when he will frequently have his bowels open, first thing in the morning and last thing at night as well. If you see him rushing around looking for a corner, take him outside, but if he hasn't been taught *why* he is being put out he will immediately become distracted and forget all about it until he comes indoors again. Dry him down thoroughly if he has been out in the wet. Never rub his nose in his mistakes, just take him to the puddle, etc., and scold verbally before taking him outside.

Coprophagy or Dirt Eating

Early habits die hard, and one of the worst of the Shih Tzu and many other breeds is eating their own excreta. This is a revolting habit which can be difficult to break. If it starts in a very young puppy, it is usually in the early hours when the litter first wakes up and they all climb out of bed to defaecate in the run. Then they start playing, there is nobody around to clean up the mess, so they play with the faeces, and from there it is a short step to getting them into their mouths and eating them. The only answer is for you to get up before the puppies, put them out if possible, but certainly clear up the mess as soon as they make it. An older puppy will sometimes start this habit and then grow out of it. The cause varies; it can sometimes be worms or it may be deficiency in the diet. The theory I hold to is the one suggested in R. H. Smythe's *The Breeding and Rearing of Dogs,* that the excreta frequently contains a large quantity of undigested protein, either because the animal has been fed too high a percentage or because this has been given in too large and concentrated a piece so that the central part has not been digested after swallowing. When in play the animal picks up the excreta, it finds the protein and then looks for more, and so the habit is formed. Some breeders find that if black treacle is added to the diet this helps, and another suggestion is to pepper the excreta, but, of course, you have to be on the spot in order to do this. Always keep the runs clean. Horse and other manure from herbivorous animals is quite a different matter. It is quite natural and normal for an animal to eat this, thereby picking up the partly digested foods containing necessary vitamins.

Daily grooming

This will not take long, but is most important even in a puppy, for it facilitates his adult grooming. Use a brush with a fairly soft bristle, and a steel comb with both fine and wide teeth.

It stimulates a puppy's coat to brush it in both directions. Either groom him on your lap or on the table; when adult, he is best groomed on the table. Although the puppy only needs a light brush and an occasional comb-through, he must be trained to lie on his back and sides to have his tummy and the insides of his thighs groomed. This should be done gently by means of both brushing and occasional combing, especially the feet as these are the parts of the body which mat most quickly and to which the animal objects most. If the puppy resents lying on his back for brushing, get him used to it by stroking his tummy. If you talk or sing to him whilst grooming, he will find this soothing.

Follow the general technique suggested in Chapter 7 dealing with the care of the coat.

Be very careful how you use the comb, as this can pull out the coat. Some people feel you should never use a comb, but I think that both you and the dog will get in a frightful mess if you don't do so!

Wash around your puppy's eyes and groom his whiskers gently every day, even if you have to miss the rest. A puppy who has been trained to grooming will look forward to this daily individual attention.

You should by now have a fairly well-trained animal. Keep up the good work, and remember that you can always go to training classes when he is older. Do not imagine that you cannot train an older Shih Tzu. This can most certainly be accomplished so long as it has had love and human contact in its early life. A dog who is using his brain is a much happier dog, and far less likely to get into mischief than one who teaches himself or learns bad habits from others.

6

General Management

Nutrition

This is one of the most important aspects of dog rearing, although there is insufficient space to deal intensively with the subject here. New knowledge of dietetics and the consequent effects on the body is constantly coming to light. With the best of intentions, much harm can be done by adding too many extras to the diet and upsetting the balance as a result.

Food consists of water, proteins, carbohydrates, fats, vitamins, minerals and amino-acids. These need to be fed in the correct proportions, since an excess of one can frequently neutralise the property of another.

The dog is a carnivorous animal, but this does not mean that it only eats large amounts of red muscle meat (correctly speaking it is an omnivora). In the wild, the dog firstly gorges itself on the vegetable protein substance of the stomach of a 'kill' before eating the entrails and offal. In this way it obtains the vital vitamins and minerals. Therefore to feed your dog entirely on red muscle meat because of its protein content is by no means sufficient.

Proteins can be given in the form of various meats, red meats such as beef and lamb and white meats such as chicken and rabbit. Other protein sources are ox cheek, sheep's head, and offals such as liver, heart and tongue. Fish, particularly herring, is good, but is very rich and cannot be given too frequently. Paunch is an excellent source of food. Lights, so frequently sold in the shops for pets, do not in fact contain much nourishment. It has been proved that dogs can thrive very well on vegetable proteins. According to McCay in *The Nutrition of the Dog,* one-fifth of the protein intake is passed out in the faeces of the dog.

Carbohydrates

It is necessary to give the Shih Tzu some form of carbohydrates, either biscuits, biscuit meal or baked brown bread, in order to ensure a balanced diet. This can be lightly soaked and fed with the meat, if only one meal a day is given, or fed dry as a separate meal. Some Shih Tzu thrive better on two meals daily rather than one, but this is something for individual owners to learn by experience. A little crisped brown bread to chew is good for the teeth, since it helps to keep them clean and prevents the accumulation of tartar. Cakes, sweets and other similar carbohydrate foods with which we are inclined to fill ourselves should not be given to dogs, although meat scraps can be utilised.

Fats

Fat is essential in a dog's diet, for it contains Vitamins A and D which are good for the coat and skin. Too much fat, however, causes nausea and vomiting.

Those are the three basic foods which, if given in variety, will ensure that the dog stands a good chance of obtaining the essential vitamins and minerals. There are, however, additional items which can benefit him if they are added, sometimes being in short supply in the normal diet.

Seaweed powder

This contains iodine, a very necessary mineral missing from some diets which also helps to grow good coats and improve pigment. One-quarter of a teaspoon can be given daily. Elderberry is also said to improve pigment.

Vitamins

The Vitamin B complex is essential to the good health of the dog, and is often lacking in the diet. It can be given in the form of Phillips' Vetzyme yeast tablets, or alternatively one teaspoon of Bemax which also contains Vitamin E (wheat germ oil).

It is suggested by McCay in *The Nutrition of the Dog* that dogs kept in cold kennels who consequently use up more carbohydrates as fuel for warmth may require extra Vitamin B. A low fat diet also requires this additive. It is suspected that the licking-up of urine indicates a lack of Vitamin B (which is passed out in the urine). Vitamin B also stimulates the appetite.

It should not be necessary to add other vitamins and minerals to the diet of healthy adult dogs under normal conditions. Good natural sources of these vitamins are egg yolk, beef liver and vegetable oils.

The coat will benefit generally if a teaspoon of corn oil or raw linseed oil is given daily, unless some form of cod liver oil is already being given. Should the dog show signs of nausea, stop the oil. This additive also helps to prevent and remove scurf.

Garlic

This is an excellent internal disinfectant and strong worm deterrent, which can be given in tablet or powder form, but few dogs will eat a crushed clove of garlic!

Vegetables

Chopped green vegetables and grated raw carrot are much appreciated, and are of great benefit.

Such fats as butter, beef fat, cream or lard will form soft fat on the dog's body. However, if the source of fat is digested carbohydrates, this will form hard fat on the body and not cause obesity.

According to Smythe in *The Breeding and Rearing of Dogs*, so-called 'chronic ear canker' responds to treatment if fat unsalted bacon or unboiled linseed oil is added to the daily feed. Conversely, a lack of this can be the cause of ear trouble. Never use rancid fats. Stale cod liver oil can become rancid if it is stored for too long, so keep it in the cool. Once the fat is rancid, Vitamins A and E will be destroyed.

Water should always be available for the dog except at the actual feeding time and up to an hour afterwards. When dry feeding, it is absolutely essential to have an adequate water supply *at all times* to replace moisture which is not in the food.

One is sometimes advised that one day's starvation in every week is beneficial, but I do not think this suits the Shih Tzu. If you are normally giving two meals daily, then you can certainly 'starve' by giving only one, but if a Shih Tzu goes too long without food, gases collect in the stomach and froth will be vomited.

If roughage is lacking in the diet, a teaspoon of bran or Allbran can be added, which should help to combat dirty trousers. If dirty trousers are frequent, it may be that the diet needs adjusting and the amount of biscuit should be increased.

Dry feeding complete meals

There are various products available on the market, and the analysis of these feeds should always be studied before they are used. Some have been used for many years, and research has proved their value. Provided they are fed correctly, dogs thrive on them.

Good husbandry

No matter how good the diet, the dog will not thrive without good husbandry. This involves regular feeds, exercise, love and attention. There are good feeders and bad feeders besides good and bad eaters. Dogs should be given their meals on separate dishes; never feed a shy dog in company with a greedy one – put the shy one in a safe compartment. Several dogs eating together usually feed better than one on its own, but conversely this may also cause them to bolt their food. Long bones can be given, but may also be the cause of a fight.

Development

Hereditary characteristics and environment go hand in hand, and feeding is a most important part of environment. According to Burns and Fraser, 'The changes in proportion undergone in a puppy during growth are regulated only partly by its breed . . . High feeding during the first three months of life tends to produce heavy bone, large feet, a long back and relatively short legs and neck, i.e. development comparable to that of early-maturing sheep' (Hammond, 1932).

The period from weaning at around eight weeks until twenty weeks of age is when pups grow most quickly. Between eight and ten weeks they consume the highest proportion of food relative to the body weight.

Heavy bone is softer and less dense than light bone, for it

bends more easily. The achrondoplastic gene (a condition in which the limbs are abnormally short) affects heavy bone rather than fine, and this makes it more difficult to get short straight legs if the bone is thick. The standard does not call for massive bone nor abnormally short legs. Great care is needed in the rearing of these dogs in order to obtain good fronts. Heavy bone is frequently the result of heavy feeding and restricted exercise. According to evidence presented by Riser (1963), heavy feeding also favours the development of hip dysplasia.

Burns and Fraser, in *Genetics of the Dog*, state that if moderate feeding up to five or six months of age is followed by heavy feeding, thickening of the long bones of the legs and coarsening of the skull are likely to result.

Rickets can also cause short, bent legs, although many knowledgeable people consider this to be a hereditary as well as a dietary condition.

It is inadvisable to follow a large meal by exercise in heavy-boned animals, since the weight of food in the stomach can cause bending of the legs. If there is a tendency for the legs to bow, it is helpful to raise the feeding bowl, etc., up off the ground to a height whereby the legs do not have to bend in order to reach it. Another precaution is to avoid walking downstairs or jumping from heights.

Results of genetical research on the conformation of the dog indicate that it is rare for a purely Mendelian factor to be involved. There can be several different causes of one specific result, i.e. 'the short leg may be due to a simple recessive gene, to partially dominant factors, to multiple factors not showing dominance, or even to rickets or to general poor nutrition', according to Burns and Fraser. Ritter stated (1937) that tooth and jaw size are inherited independently of each other.

Under-feeding will produce faulty, weedy bodies which are prone to disease, and this practice should never be employed in the misguided idea that it will restrict an animal's size.

To date there have unfortunately been no scientific studies regarding the influence of nutrition on conformation. However, I hope that the above information will help people to realise that the growth of the puppy depends as much on satisfactory environment as on good breeding.

At four months of age a puppy has reached approximately

half his adult weight, and by six months two-thirds of the adult weight. Factors of size and weight should always be considered in conjunction.

Exercise

Never force a puppy under six months of age to go for long walks on the lead; short lead walks are all right for a little training, but most of the exercise should be taken free, in the garden, or if out walking allow him to stop and rest whenever he feels tired. Should the puppy be destined for a show career, then it is unwise to allow too much romping around, but he should not be so restricted that he does not have the opportunity to extend the limbs and tighten the muscles. Remember that puppy bones are soft – never let a puppy stand up too much on his hind legs in order to watch what is going on, for he will tend to balance with his toes turned in and this may make him cow-hocked.

The adult Shih Tzu needs adequate exercise to keep him in a healthy, hard condition, and a show dog in particular should have regular road walking.

Shih Tzu are normally great walkers, and I hope this feature will remain with the breed. I have known many who exercise freely with the horses, as I have said, and they are certainly capable of exercise with the most active breeds such as gundogs, sheep-dogs, whippets and Alsatians. They may be animated doormats at home, but can be veritable whirlwinds when out running, to the amazement of people who have stated that they would not be seen dead at the other end of a lead! It is amazing how much they will exercise themselves, indoors or out, by rushing round and round dodging obstacles.

I have only mentioned road walking as a necessity for the show dog, but the pet dog loves a country ramble; do not go in the heat of a summer's day, for their heavy coats will make them uncomfortably hot. However, the pet seldom carries the long, heavy coat of the show dog, as it either becomes rubbed off, combed out or cut down. Very long-coated dogs cannot be walked in rough country because the coat gathers up too many twigs.

Wet weather

The Shih Tzu gets very dirty when out for a walk in the wet, and the easiest way to deal with this is to have a large bowl and cloth available on return and to wipe the undercarriage, wringing out the cloth in clean water and then removing the surplus moisture. Rinse each leg in turn in the water, gently pressing out the wet. If the dog is soaked, the use of newspaper for a preliminary mopping-up operation will save your towels!

In summer

Do be very careful not to exercise the dogs where there are grass seeds. Wild barley is the worst in this respect, for it works its way right through the coat and can lodge in the skin, particularly in such areas as the soft skin of the armpits, where if it gets under the surface an abscess may result. Grass seeds can also get into the ears, up the nose and between the pads, and in all these places can be extremely troublesome to the dog.

In snow

The Shih Tzu loves to play in the snow, and is a very pretty sight to watch. However, he is *not* a pretty sight when he comes in from play! He will be freezing cold with snow 'balling' all over him, up his legs, under his tummy, just about everywhere. If he is a show dog, care must be exercised in removing the snow, because unless it is thawed off the ends of the hair are likely to be broken. Stand him in a shallow bath of tepid water, and literally bathe the snow off. Better still, prevent it from happening in the first place by lightly smearing the vulnerable parts (e.g., feet, legs and stomach) with cooking oil. The snow will not stick to this.

By the sea

Sea water is not good for a dog's coat, especially since he will come straight out of the water, and roll in the sand; this is liable to get into his eyes, and to irritate the skin, making him scratch sore places which can lead to eczema. Keep him under reasonable control on the beach, and if he does get wet and sandy rinse him thoroughly when you get home.

Be careful if you are near a fast-flowing river, for many Shih Tzu are great water dogs and will jump in.

Dentition

The Shih Tzu is sometimes late in cutting his teeth, though some lines are later than others. Many do not have their first incisors through by eight weeks, nor their second teeth by six months. Dogs should have a total of 28 temporary teeth and 42 permanent teeth: 20 in the upper jaw and 22 in the lower, consisting of 6 incisors, 2 canines, 8 premolars and 6 molars.

In the brachycephalic (short-faced) breeds, teeth and jaws frequently prove to be a problem, so extra care in this respect is a good precaution.

Of the front teeth, the four canines or eye teeth appear before the incisors, which can, however, be felt long before they actually erupt from the gum.

At around four to five months of age, the pup's milk teeth will be shed, though one or two are sometimes left in the jaw and these may push the permanent teeth out of place. It is wise to check on this, and to have these puppy teeth removed if they do not come out naturally of their own accord; there will then be room for the permanent teeth to come through in the correct position.

Teeth can be cleaned by rubbing them with a piece of cloth wrapped round your finger. You can use warm water, a saline solution, or a 1-in-10 solution of bicarbonate of soda. The latter helps to remove any odour or yellow discolouration. Take care that tartar is not allowed to form round the teeth, for this will get under the gum and can cause premature loosening of the teeth. In some cases it may be necessary for the vet to remove tartar under anaesthetic. You can avoid these problems by making sure that the dog is not fed on sloppy foods and giving him a hard biscuit to chew – most dogs like a 'bonio'. Bones are a controversial item, but these hard foods do help to keep tartar away. Recently a toothpaste called 'Showrite' has come on the market; this is marketed by Crooks and keeps teeth clear of tartar if used regularly. Do not worry if puppies go off their food at teething times, this is to be expected as their gums are bound to be sore.

Internal parasites

Roundworms. These are the common internal parasites found in puppies. A puppy can be born with them, for the worm ova is passed to him in the bloodstream of the bitch. In this country a young puppy seldom suffers from any other variety of worms. When first acquiring your puppy, be sure to ascertain whether or not it has been wormed by the breeder. Roundworms vary in length and look like white garden worms; perhaps an even better description may be to say they look like pieces of spaghetti. If worming has not been done, get tablets from your veterinary surgeon. Small puppies can be infected with worms without showing any of the symptoms, i.e. an indifferent or variable appetite, poor coat, general unthrifty appearance, a pot belly which feels tight and hard. Other symptoms may be running eyes and nose, a cough and a depraved appetite (i.e. eating excreta). There may be straining to pass a motion, which is frequently loose and contains mucus. If the worms get into the stomach, the puppy may vomit them. It is not difficult to worm a dog; starving is quite unnecessary nowadays, and the appropriate pill can be given with the food and seldom upsets the animal.

Should there be a toddler in the house, worming really is vital from all viewpoints, for a small child is liable to pick up a puppy's toy and stick it into his own mouth.

Although I have emphasised the importance of worming, do not become over-preoccupied with this problem. As with so many things, prevention is better than cure, and early worming should avoid most of the problems described. A healthy adult should become immune to this parasite, and throw out the ova before they have a chance to hatch. This in turn needs watching, however, for the adult will pass the ova in a stool, and it then lies around on the grass, hence frequent re-infestation can occur.

Tapeworms. These are segmented, narrowing towards the head, and the latter must be passed in a motion or the worm simply starts to grow again. This parasite requires an intermediate host, one example of which is the flea. An animal suffering from tapeworm frequently passes segments in its stool; these are flat and oval, resembling small pieces of dried rice, and can be seen sticking to the underpart of the tail. It is advisable to obtain suitable pills from your veterinary surgeon. Treatment is quite simple, and no longer has adverse effects as in former times.

External parasites

Fleas. The flea does not lay its eggs on the dog's body, but in nooks and crannies in articles such as bedding, also in the grass. The eggs develop into maggots and in turn into fleas which jump on to the nearest available living animal. Dog fleas do not as a rule remain on humans. This parasite is more likely to attack the young and old, the sick and unhealthy animals. Intense irritation will be caused by even one flea on a normally clean dog. Treatment for an adult involves dusting with a gammexane powder such as Pulvex, or a similar proprietary brand. These powders are poisonous, and while quite safe for older animals should never be used on puppies or nursing bitches. Derris or pyrethrum may be used on puppies; where a nursing bitch is concerned, it is wise to seek your vet's advice. It is my personal experience that powder falls out of the coat too easily in the Shih Tzu, and if powdering several dogs – which is likely, for if one has a flea there is every chance the others have too – the powder gets into the air, when the effect of inhaling it is unpleasant and irritating to the mucous membranes, especially if one suffers from any kind of allergy, hay fever, etc. I prefer to bathe the dogs with a special shampoo; use either Seleen suspension (made by Messrs. Abbot Ltd.) or a proprietary insecticidal shampoo, for this purpose. Many germicidal shampoos do not kill fleas or lice, although they act as a good deterrent.

Lice. These are very small and grey in colour, although they can be seen by the naked eye; they do not jump, but burrow their heads into the dog. They live their cycle on the host, and do not transfer to humans, but may transfer from one dog to another when there are several in close contact with each other; therefore, all the dogs who are together in a group will need treating. The eggs are laid on the sides of the hairs and look like small particles of scurf, but unlike scurf will not brush off and need to be removed with a special fine comb. The dog requires four regular weekly treaments to rid it of lice, the life cycle of the louse, from egg to adult, being two to four weeks. Bathing with the above-mentioned shampoos is satisfactory, alternatively you can obtain a special preparation from your veterinarian Although it is a fairly easy matter to rid one or two dogs of these pests, it is quite a different matter bathing a large number once a week for a month. Infestation should be avoided.

After treating your dogs, it is essential to prevent re-infestation by both fleas and lice. Burn all bedding and dust over all beds with a suitable powder – your vet will advise on this. Be particularly careful to treat kennels, especially the corners and crevices; the easiest way to achieve this is to spray with a preparation which will kill parasites and their ova. Cromosal Ltd. of Glasgow market one such preparation, which should be available from your pet store. Also, it is possible to hire appliances which can be wired into the nearest electric point, and burn capsules to kill all such pests (e.g. Aerovap).

Inoculations

It is *most important* to have your puppy immunised against distemper, hard pad, canine virus hepatitis and leptrospiral jaundice. Two injections are usually given, the first between eight and twelve weeks of age, depending on your veterinary surgeon and the type of vaccine used, the second about two weeks later.

Young puppies should not mix with other dogs (apart, obviously, from their litter mates) or be handled by other dog-owners before inoculation is completed. Should the vaccines be given whilst the puppy is already incubating a disease, they can have adverse results. Neither should a young pup be taken out until he has gained some immunity, which is generally reckoned to be fourteen days after the final injection. A booster dose should be given annually, although some vets consider this unnecessary in show animals whom, they feel, develop their own immunity. Your own veterinarian is the one to advise you in this matter.

Insurance

You may wish to insure your puppy, and a fully comprehensive insurance will also cover a large proportion of the vet's fees. There are certain firms who deal specifically with dog insurance, for example the Canine and Livestock Insurance Association Ltd., of Calia House, 24–26 Spring Street, London, W.2, and the Dog Breeders Insurance Co. Ltd., of Beacon House, Lansdowne, Bournemouth, Hants. Fully comprehensive insurance can be expensive, and the Shih Tzu is a very robust little dog. It is important that you should have third-party cover, for if your dog gets out on the road and causes an accident you are liable by law, and this could involve you in great expense with legal costs; insurance premiums (for third party only) to protect you against this eventuality are low.

Kennels and runs

There is no doubt that the ideal way to keep the Shih Tzu is in the house as a companion, and this is usually quite practicable with small numbers. In this way, their characters are fully developed and they are best able to get all the attention they need.

Now that the breed is better known and becoming so popular, more and more breeders are taking it up, either to start a new kennel or as a second string to an existing kennel. I feel some information and advice should therefore be given regarding the care of the Shih Tzu in kennels.

The breed can be kept in outside kennels perfectly happily so long as it is catered for correctly. It is an intensely curious and lively little creature, and to shut it away in a kennel while you go off to work is nothing short of mental cruelty. All kennel dogs should be given the opportunity to spend a certain amount of time in the home as well, especially bitches in whelp who need extra love, and nursing mothers. Please bring all your dogs into the home occasionally, even if they sleep outside; this will give them the chance to have the closer contact with the human family which they need, and which is indeed a hereditary right so far as the Shih Tzu is concerned.

Kennels should be situated near or adjacent to the house, where the dogs can be both seen and heard, and where they can hear your call and be aware of your presence. To have the kennels close by is to your advantage as well as theirs, for there

Ch. Ellingham Kala Nag. Oil painting by Truda Panet, 1963

(Alison Snell)

Ch. Newroots Nankipoo of Snaefell at ten months

Ch. Lochranza Choo Ling
of Cathay

(Diane Pearce)

Ch. Cherholmes Golden
Samantha

(Diane Pearce)

Ch. Mu T'Ang of Antarct-
ica

(Diane Pearce)

are times they may need attention at night. In the daytime you can watch them in their runs, and it is a great help to be able to observe the progress of your young stock. There is also much pleasure to be gained in watching them at play.

With this breed there is a great temptation to keep it too closely confined, with the aim of growing a coat and cutting down on the amount of work entailed when the dog leads a normal life.

It is far better to have a larger-sized kennel, which can be sub-divided if necessary, than a tiny kennel which is not only difficult to clean out but quite inadequate for the dog when shut in. The heat in a small wooden kennel, for example, on a summer's day – and we do get them occasionally – can be quite over-powering. If it is necessary for the dog to be confined to its kennel, even for short periods, this should be insulated and should have shuttered windows which can be opened at floor level.

Several Shih Tzu can be kept together, although there will frequently be one very jealous dog or a stud dog who is 'kennel boss'. It is always wise to have more kennel accommodation available than you would normally require, enabling you to keep any trouble-makers or coat-chewers apart, or to separate them in cases of infection; ample accommodation also facilitates disinfection and annual treatment and repair of the kennels.

I prefer to keep my bitches who are in season well away from the stud dogs, which prevents the latter from becoming troublesome and losing weight. There is nothing like the proximity of bitches in season to cause fighting amongst stud dogs.

If you can provide several kennels with separate runs, plus one large exercising area, this will keep the dogs more lively for they can be moved from one to the other; this not only adds a spice of interest to their lives, but is particularly beneficial if you are unable to take them out for daily walks, for without help daily exercising is not always possible with a number of dogs.

The Shih Tzu can be kept alongside most other breeds, especially the gun dogs and working breeds. This is the life the Shih Tzu likes, with the opportunity to go out with his active companions.

Never shut your Shih Tzu away in a cage and leave them to sit around for hours on end; they may end up with excellent coats, but extremely poor bodies and action, quite apart from the fact

G

that you will also cause much mental cruelty. You may fool some of the judges some of the time, but never all the judges all the time! The body underneath the coat and the action of the dog are of vital importance to this breed, and these can only be achieved by good kennelling and management. Coats which trail along the ground are quite unnecessary. Always remember that the dog should be 'lively, alert and active'.

Kennel runs

If you keep your dogs in the house and have an enclosed garden then you are indeed fortunate. However, if you have an open garden, as I have, looking out onto a busy main road, then certain measures have to be taken, and if you have outside kennelling then you will also need runs. I think it is a mistake to run dogs solely on one type of surface, whether that surface is grass or concrete. Use of grass means that it is absolutely essential to walk the dog daily on a hard, rough surface. Cement or concrete runs, which are favoured by most people because of the ease of cleaning, also have snags. They hold the water and can stay damp for some time, so in this case benches should be provided for the dogs to sit on. There is no 'give' in concrete, and although it is a good – if rough – surface for bringing a dog up on its toes, too much movement in this respect can weaken the pasterns.

Some makes of porous cement slabs are good, such as the Sussex Slab made by Thakeham; another is made by Garden Stone of Naphill, High Wycombe. However, others, particularly the pumice slabs, are too rough and tear the coat. These porous slabs should be laid loose on a sand base for drainage.

Shingle of a medium size – about 4 in deep – is good for the feet; the dogs soon become accustomed to it, and will happily run around and play on it. Although cheaper than concrete, it does need constant replacement, for some will be removed with the faeces every time they are cleared up. Shingle drains well, but the dogs can dig in it and scatter pebbles in all directions.

Clinker runs are very good for the feet, but a dog should not be left in this type of run for too long. Digging to Australia is a lovely game! My little Me Wun dug a hole one foot deep by one foot wide, and then had a great game enticing her puppy to it and pushing him in. Shih Tzu can dig with their mouths as well as with their feet, and it is no good grumbling that your dogs have no whiskers left if you allow them to dig!

The best answer I have come up with for runs is to have as many and varied types of surface as possible, which seems to work but does require the use of more space.

Remember that grass runs must be limed once a year, and even this does not completely eradicate worm ova. Clear away all excreta, remembering that in wet weather slugs attack the faeces and that slugs in turn bring lice.

Kennel cleaning

Kennels need cleaning out daily, although I find that most Shih Tzu are very clean in their kennels. Ample fresh water should always be available, and the containers must be washed out and refilled rather than merely topped up. Apart from daily cleaning they should be scrubbed weekly, particular attention being paid to cracks and crevices; use a disinfectant, but please be careful that this is made up in the correct strength. Too strong a disinfectant has been known to cause sterility. I put Vynol flooring down in all my kennels, which is easy to wash over, and I also spray all walls and floors monthly with a special disinfectant to minimise the risk of parasites.

Fencing

On the whole, fencing is not too difficult with the Shih Tzu, but if you have a naughty one or a persistent escapist, then you need to take special precautions. I find 4 ft chain-link fencing satisfactory; ordinary wire netting can be used, but it does not last. I use 6-foot-high fencing for my bitches in season, but even this height can be insufficient without extra guard rails round the top if there are any straying labradors around. I once had four bitches in season together inside their 6-foot-high run, and on hearing a frightful noise went to investigate, only to find a labrador amongst them. From the reception he received I think he was sorry he'd ever jumped in, but once inside he found it difficult to jump out!

The netting should be securely sunk into the ground. I have

some bitches who can get out of most things, by chewing through wood or wire, digging under and climbing over, and these determinedly naughty ones invariably end up in the house. Just as with humans, it doesn't seem to pay to be good! We also get the persistent burrower, who will tunnel a way under any shed which is not on a fully cemented base.

Heating and lighting

It is a very great help to have electricity laid on to your kennels, and in the winter lighting is virtually essential. Whether or not the kennels should be heated is a controversial point. If unheated, then they should be lined and insulated. This insulation is equally important in summer and winter since, as mentioned earlier, heat can become intense. Any heating must be of a very safe nature; electricity is by far the best, and I prefer a thermostatic-controlled electrically-heated oil radiator. It is only necessary to use this in very cold or wet weather, for once they are past puppy stage the dogs do not required much heat. Some centrally heated homes are too hot for their comfort.

Litter and bedding

Never, on any account, use sawdust on the floor. This gets into the coat, and when the Shih Tzu relieves himself he frequently scratches the ground with his back legs. What with this and shaking himself, sawdust ends up in the eyes and the next thing is an eye ulcer.

I would never recommend the use of wood wool for bedding for a Shih Tzu; this gets into the coat and tangles up the hair. Small pieces can break off, bury themselves up to the skin and cause intense irritation. The same argument applies to straw. I do not think there is any better bedding than plenty of newspapers, since this is both warm and absorbent, and can be easily burned. The only disadvantage, so far as I am aware, is that the print is liable to brush off on to a white dog.

The elderly animal

The Shih Tzu is a long-lived dog; it has been known to live

to 21 years, and many live to be 16. Generally speaking, the breed remains lively and youthful into old age, and the dog who has led an active and regular life, with sensible feeding, is likely to show the benefit when getting old.

However, the old dog will naturally slow down, and it is necessary to keep his life well regulated. He should still have adequate exercise, although this may have to take a different form. If the dog does not get taken out it will be inclined to sleep all day, becoming fatter, stiffer and in softer condition. My experience of elderly Shih Tzu is that they become greedier and greedier, and I have ten veterans myself at the time of writing this book.

Do ensure that the older dog has a large enough bed, and that this is free from draughts. Although warmth is appreciated, don't permit your dog to sit too close to the fire or stove; this will only cause skin trouble, to which old dogs are more prone in any case without any extra help.

Regular grooming will keep the skin in condition. Otherwise it is inclined to become scurfy and rather dry. A little extra corn oil or linseed oil in the food will help to combat dryness, and if the skin and coat are generally in poor condition rubbing in a little coconut oil will help.

Teeth. Have teeth checked regularly; decaying ones should be removed, for they can poison the whole system.

Diet. This largely depends on the dog's general condition. If he is showing no signs of failing digestion, such as vomiting or diarrhoea, bringing up wind or vomiting froth, you can keep to the normal diet. Otherwise a failing digestion may need veterinary advice regarding suitable feeding.

Body Odour. If older dogs are not regularly groomed they are inclined to smell 'doggy'. Careful grooming will help considerably by cleaning the skin of its debris, and it is also helpful to rub over the coat with a chlorophyll cloth afterwards. I have never found any harm come to older dogs through bathing them, so long as care is taken to keep them warm until they are absolutely dry.

The Senses. Sight is usually the first sense to fail with the Shih Tzu. A blind dog is quite happy so long as it remains in familiar surroundings, and it is surprising how well it manages to get around. If trouble is caused by discharge from the eyes, bathe them daily. It can also be helpful to cut away the hair around them, thus preventing the possibility of friction on the cornea. Always be cautious when you approach a blind animal – speak its name and let it sniff the back of your hand before touching it.

A deaf dog should also be approached gently, for any sudden movement can startle it and make it nervy. Never allow young children to worry old dogs, particularly when they are sleeping.

Some diseases of old age

Pyometra is inflammation of the womb, and is a common problem in old bitches who have seldom or never been bred from, particularly those who have had false pregnancies. An over-long season is a forerunner of this condition, and abnormal discharge is a bad sign. An operation for the removal of the womb and ovaries is the best cure; the bitch recovers remarkably quickly, and regains an amazing amount of youthfulness as a result. You will not help to prevent this condition by 'just letting the bitch have one litter, to do her good'.

Lumps are developed by many old dogs in various parts of the body. In bitches, these frequently appear on the mammary glands, but since they seldom cause trouble they are usually left alone provided they do not seem to be unduly increasing in size. Veterinary advice should be sought.

Heart disease is another frequent cause for concern. The first obvious sign of this is usually a hard, dry cough, and veterinary advice should be sought immediately.

Diabetes may also affect old animals. Symptoms are excessive drinking, vomiting, possible loss of appetite and an enlarged abdomen, which gives the owner a misguided picture of fatness whilst the ribs and vertebrae are horribly prominent. Insulin injections can be given, but treatment by mouth is unsatisfactory. If the dog objects to the injection it may be kinder to have it humanely destroyed.

Failing kidneys appear to be one of the more frequent causes of premature ageing and death in the Shih Tzu, sometimes arising out of an earlier infection. Inflammation of the kidney can be brought on by damp, or if the dog gets chilled, older dogs being much more likely to suffer from the effects than young ones. Excessive thirst and frequent passing of urine are early signs of trouble, but if a specimen of urine is immediately taken to the vet for examination and tests, serious trouble may be averted; a special diet may have to be given, consisting mainly of milky puddings, Benger's food, malt and cod liver oil, dog biscuit, condensed milk and Virol, with no red meats or eggs.

Rheumatic conditions can also be caused by damp, and the dog will become very stiff. It will be necessary to provide a bed where he can stretch out at full length, otherwise if he lies on the floor he will be open to draughts.

Bladder weakness is something which may affect old dogs, particularly if they have been castrated or spayed. The only remedy I can suggest is to let them out more frequently, and to put newspaper by the door when you have to leave them for any length of time.

Symptoms of age must be treated as they arise; do not treat an ageing dog as old before it is necessary to do so, just take sensible precautions to avert trouble. There are special liver and kidney tablets for older dogs, which act as very good tonics; these can be obtained from your veterinary surgeon.

Bitches continue with their seasons for varying ages; the length of each season shortens, and it may occur only once a year. Stud dogs can continue to sire good litters of puppies well into old age, provided they are in good health.

Always dry down an old dog thoroughly when he comes in from the wet, and do not let him sit around on damp surfaces such as grass and concrete, which retain moisture. Damp in itself is a predisposing cause of many ills.

The nails of an older animal also need special care, and may require trimming because a reduced amount of exercise means that they are less likely to get worn down.

Never let an old dog suffer unnecessarily, but ask your veterinarian to put it to sleep; this is done by injection, and is quick and painless. See this act through yourself for your friend, and don't let the veterinarian take him away alone to end his life in the surgery without friends. Have it done at home, where – lying quietly in the arms of the master or mistress he adores – his short life on this earth can peacefully be ended.

7

Care of the Coat

To the showman, the beauty of the Shih Tzu shines forth in his coat. To the pet owner, the coat can be a deterrent. Never glamourise the coat to the disadvantage of character, soundness and health.

The beautiful coat does require care and attention. It is not difficult to keep two or three Shih Tzu in perfect condition, but it is very hard work to keep more than this number well groomed, especially if you have another breed to care for as well.

Moulting occurs in bitches twice a year, and in dogs usually only once. The guard hairs of the coat do not fall out. The underwool only is shed, but this does not fall out either. Great attention to grooming is needed during this period, or the dead coat will mat into thick wads of wool. This eventuality will be dealt with later in the chapter.

As stated, all colours are permissible, but fading genes make it difficult to breed for colour. The changing colour is noticeable even in the adult coat, and adds to the interest and beauty of the Shih Tzu appearance-

The coat is not dead straight, as in a Yorkshire terrier, but (as mentioned in the chapter on Standards) while a slight wave is permitted a curl is not acceptable. A natural parting falls down the back.

A very brittle coat will break easily, and is more inclined to curl. A great deal of attention is required in order to get it back into condition. Some stripping out may even be necessary, followed by careful treatment of the new growth. Additional vegetable oil in the diet may help, and a light smear of almond oil can be applied during grooming, about three times a week.

A healthy coat requires a healthy body, and as in humans the hair of a sick dog will be adversely affected. Good feeding and management are essential for a good coat.

Types and coat colours

Different coloured coats carry different textures, some being stronger and easier to grow and manage than others.

Black and white is very smart and eye-catching, but has its disadvantages. In some lines the puppy black fades to grey, and in any case the black is frequently soft and difficult to grow, increasing at a different rate from the white and thus leaving the dog shorter in coat where the black grows. The two colours also vary in texture, and black and white specimens sometimes carry a very woolly undercoat.

Brindle shades, although these usually change their colour with age, produce coats of a good strong texture, carrying a good undercoat, which is generally very manageable.

Golds come in numerous shades from pastel shades and pale honey to deep red-gold and chestnut.

There are known to be at least two gene groups for gold. One is for the browns, dull golds and livers, which frequently lack black pigment and may have off-black noses. Liver is the same as black with the exception of the one missing pigment. The other group covers yellows, apricots and clear bright golds; these carry full black pigment, and the solid golds have black masks while most of the others have white. Both are permissible, but black masks have the advantage of keeping cleaner – or at least appearing to do so!

The texture of the gold coat varies with the shade. Pastel shades grow thick and strong, with good undercoats, whereas the true gold is slow to mature and frequently carries less undercoat – it is soft, and more care is required in grooming.

A colour which is rarely seen is the 'blue' – as of the Persian cat – which carries a grey nose and light grey eye. It will probably be a year or two before this colour is recognised and fully appreciated, and perhaps used in colour breeding. At present, animals with this colouring are sold as pets.

I have also known of a true black and tan marking, black bodies with gold points and 'four eyes'.

Silver appears to be closely connected to gold.

Tools

Good grooming is essential to stimulate the hair growth and keep the dog's coat in a healthy condition.

Most breeders have their own pet methods of grooming, and some use the comb very little while others use it all the time. Both seem to achieve beautiful coats on their dogs, which just proves that there can be no hard and fast rules. I will put forward a suitable method from my own viewpoint, and you will have to learn by experience whether this is best for you personally. So much is up to you, the owner, and the way the tools are used.

Combs. The type I prefer is a steel comb with wide teeth one end and fine teeth the other. I consider it essential to use this, for the dead hair in the coat must be combed out, but it should be used gently or you can drag out too much undercoat and break the ends of the guard hairs. Never try to drag out the mats with your comb, this will only hurt the dog and cause him to dislike his grooming.

Brushes. I consider that the type of brush used should vary with different coats. The wire brush is to be frowned upon, in my opinion, and should only be used when the coat has unfortunately become out of hand, for the wires can scratch the dog's skin in a most uncomfortable manner. I find that the most satisfactory brush for a dog in a full coat of strong texture is the Maison Pearson nylon and bristle, which will get right through the coat without damage or injury. For softer, finer coats I prefer the old-fashioned bristle hair brush, now hard to come by – alas – but sometimes to be obtained at market stalls and jumble sales. One can spend a lot of money on brushes which turn out to be quite useless. For the puppy, a soft bristle hairbrush is all that is needed.

Method

A quick groom and a face wash should be carried out daily, with a thorough grooming once a week.

When the puppy is small, grooming can be done on your lap, but as he grows it is best done on the table where he can be taught to stand up. Always use the same place for grooming, and the dog will become accustomed to it.

Be regular, and use brush and comb to give the dog a thorough 'going-over' once a week, between times using the brush only. Even if you do not have time to groom every day, always make time to clean round the dog's eyes.

If you are gentle, and never pull the hair unnecessarily, the dog will enjoy the attention you are giving him and will allow you to tease out any mats and snarls. Accustom your puppy to grooming at an early age, training him to lie down so that his underside can be done. Cut the elastic band which ties the top-knot – you will lose less hair this way. Groom with a wet spray – either rain water for preference, or one of the many coat conditioners available from your pet shop.

Do not forget to condition the coat – some coats are very brittle, but as mentioned in the previous chapter, the dog may need one teaspoon of corn oil, unboiled linseed oil or some other fat with his food. Brittle coats break easily, whereas the slightly greasy coat grows strongly.

If your Shih Tzu gets taken out for rough walking in the country, it is best to go over his coat thoroughly afterwards, using the comb where necessary, for he is sure to get twigs, leaves and burrs (and, during the summer, grass seeds) stuck in his coat. If these are left in they will make the coat more tangled than ever, and by working their way up to the skin surface will cause irritation and scratching.

Weekly grooming

Head. Wash round the dog's eyes with warm water, saline solution, Optrex or weak tea, removing any discharge or matter which may have collected. If the eyes are neglected, matter will collect in the corners by the nose; this discharge can not only rot the hair but also make a sore place on the flesh. It is helpful to rub a little Vaseline round the eyes. If matting has occurred, do not drag it away with the comb, for you will pull all the hair as well, and this will be very painful to the dog; instead, tease the tangles with your fingers and thumb to loosen them and then soften with water. If persistent, treat with an 'anti-mat' lotion as described in the following section on the *Body.* A drop of Optrex can be put into the eyes.

Wash the beard and whiskers, then comb gently. The best time for this is after feeding, thus removing any food deposits which may have collected under the chin. Some foods stain the whiskers.

Brush and comb the ears downwards, not forgetting the area under the ear flaps which is a bad place for matting. See that the ears are clean, and that the hair which grows inside them is not caked up with wax. This hair should periodically be pulled gently out.

At about five months the hair on top of the head will have grown long enough to tie up, which prevents it from falling into the eyes, mouth and food. Comb it up from the stop of the nose and fix it in a small elastic band. Be careful not to get other hair

Figure 11 Tying the top-knot

caught up in it, nor to draw the hair up too tightly thus pulling up the eyes. If you cut the top-knot – which should never be done in a show dog – be careful to cut so that the hair does not fall into the eyes; either make it short as in a puppy, or allow it to fall over the top of the eyes. The dog can see through this fall of hair, and it will give protection when in rough country.

Body. Make the dog lie down, then part and layer his coat while you brush him all over.

Brush from the skin outwards, and then use the comb. This is necessary, for if you only brush the top surface you will not remove the dead hair, which will mat and felt. A dog who is matted underneath presents a very bulky appearance, and this also prevents the new coat from growing. Whilst grooming, there is a good opportunity to make sure that there are no signs of parasites. Fleas can be picked up from the grass very easily during the summer months.

Always brush in the direction the hair grows; if you brush upwards you are more likely to pull out too much undercoat. Do not use too fine a comb, as this also removes an excess of undercoat.

If the dog has any persistent mats or snarls, use one of the useful 'anti-mat' preparations which can be obtained from dog beauty parlours or stalls at the dog shows. Put a little of the lotion on to the mat, working it in with your thumb and finger, then gently ease the hair apart; the guard hairs should then slip out of the mat, and you can comb them through gently. Some hair will be inevitably lost in this process, but it should not show. If the tangle has become so bad that you cannot work it with your fingers, and it must be cut, then use pointed scissors and cut from the skin outwards along the way of the hair. You will lose more hair than by the teasing process, but at least it will hang correctly. *Never cut across the coat.*

Brush the dog's stomach while he is lying down on his side, which you will have taught him to do as a puppy. You can now go over the inside of his legs and under his armpits, two places where mats are always more likely to appear. Use your brush gently on his tummy, for it is tender. A dog should have his undercarriage sponged frequently, for this will keep him smelling sweet.

The trousers need careful attention should they have become soiled. If droppings have stuck to them these may have become caked on, and the Shih Tzu has a way of trying to clean himself which only presses the dirt more firmly into the trousers! Prevention is better than cure here, so adjust his diet or add a dessertspoon of bran or Allbran. This will help to add bulk and soak up the moisture in the intestines.

Attend to the feet carefully, for they are sensitive. The lower leg and the feet mat easily, these being the parts which most frequently get wet. Do not catch your comb in the dew claws. Hair grows on the foot between the pads, and this needs watching because if the dog is always on grass it can grow too long and become twisted up around the pads. It can also ball up with mud or little stones, and can be painful enough to cause lameness. Soak the hair and work or cut out the mats, whichever process worries the dog least. Keep a check on the nails, which should be kept short; if the dog is walking on hard surfaces he will probably keep them down himself, but he cannot wear down his dew claws. For further details, see the next section.

Anal Glands. Some people consider that the anal glands should be regularly squeezed as a periodical addition to the grooming; these two little glands are situated on either side inside the anus, and sometimes become congested. Squeezing can harm the surrounding tissues, however, and this should not be done unless absolutely necessary. It is safest to ask your vet's opinion, and he will squeeze them for you if he thinks it is advisable.

Groom carefully, systematically and regularly all over, and your dog will look forward to this time with you and the attention he gets. If you have several dogs they will practically queue up for their turn!

This is the full weekly groom; for the daily groom you should attend to the head, and just brush the body over lightly. This is best done with the dog standing on the table.

For show dogs with some types of coats, a daily brushing may be too much. In such cases, three times a week may well be sufficient, especially with the black and white coat, but the head should still be attended to daily.

Talk to your dog while he is being groomed, for he finds this soothing and enjoys it.

Nails. Dealing with the nails can be a painful operation, and a dog which has once been hurt will always make a fuss. There is a section of 'quick' running down the nail, and you must avoid this when clipping; if you should inadvertently cut it, bleeding will occur and it will be very painful. One is usually well advised to keep a styptic handy, such as tinct. benzoin co. (Friar's Balsam) or permanganate of potash crystals. I would suggest that you cut the nail slightly less than necessary rather than risk cutting the quick and making it bleed.

Some nails are black and others are pink. With a pink nail you can easily see the pink quick, but it is not so easy to pick this out on the black nail, therefore it is advisable to cut off only the nail tip. I think the guillotine clippers or dew claw clippers are the least painful, as they do not squash the nail together. If the 'quick' has grown too long to cut the nail, filing is best. File from the base to the tip.

With a puppy, I hold him firmly in my left arm, holding out the paw with my left hand, but if he struggles then assistance is necessary. You need to cut in a good light, for there is so much fur around the tiny claw and it must be done very carefully. Ordinary nail scissors may be used.

When manicuring an adult dog, I prefer to cut the nails without assistance, unless the dog is particularly difficult, for I feel that an animal which is being firmly held by someone else becomes frightened and immediately begins to struggle. I make my dogs sit on the table in a good light, then pick up the paws one by one and just cut. They have been accustomed to this from puppyhood and have not been unduly hurt, so they seldom struggle.

The dew claws must be checked very carefully, for fur can easily mat around these, and the comb can get caught in them during grooming. If allowed to grow long, they are liable to continue growing round in a circle, piercing and continuing to grow into the pad. This must be most painful, and is likely to cause lameness. Dew claws are a nuisance, and although they may have been thought lucky by the Chinese they usually prove unlucky to the dog. Therefore it is best to have them removed when the whelp is only three days old.

Bathing

This is a controversial subject. Some people say it removes too much of the natural oil from the coat, and should only be done when absolutely necessary. Certainly a white dog will get dirty much more quickly after a bath, and good regular grooming can keep most Shih Tzu clean and fresh. So much depends on where you live and the type of life the dog leads. Clay soil will brush out of the coat quite easily. My dogs get filthy, and certainly need bathing, as they roll in our black sandy soil which works right into the coat and is inclined to stick.

During the summer months it is a wise precaution to give a monthly bath to all dogs who run on grass, using a germicidal shampoo as a preventative against any parasites.

The first bath should be given with great care. Puppies can be bathed from eight weeks, if necessary, but it is essential to see that they are thoroughly dry and remain in a warm room for several hours afterwards. A sink can be used when bathing a puppy, making it easier to control and less frightening for the animal. If it is frightened on the first occasion there may always be trouble. The same method is used for bathing an adult.

Never bath a dog which is in moult if you can avoid doing so, and in any case carry out a thorough grooming first.

Use a good dog shampoo, or even a baby shampoo. A special rinse for putting body into the coat, or for preventing matting, can be used to advantage and obtained from a good pet store.

To prevent water from getting into the ears, put in cotton wool before bathing. Use pieces which are large enough to be removed easily afterwards.

Always use a non-slip mat in the bath, or the dog will slip and slide around; this can not only be very frightening, particularly to a puppy, but will make your task more difficult. Leave the plug out and have water running all the time. Do not fill the bath so that the dog is virtually swimming.

First of all, wet the coat thoroughly all over, which in a full-coated dog like the Shih Tzu can take quite a bit of doing! Always wet the head last, holding it backwards with the ear flaps held down firmly against the side of the head and spraying the front.

Give the coat two good lathers, with a rinse in between. Be careful not to get soap in the eyes or water in the ears. After the second lather, rinse very well in order to make quite sure you have got all the soap out. In a hard-water area this is not always so easy, and if you can use rain water you will be wise to do so. Then rub in any special rinse, leaving it for the required time before rinsing it off.

Wipe the surplus water off the coat with your hands, then dry the dog thoroughly with a towel. Do not rub in a circular action, for this will mat up the undercoat. Then let him have a good shake

Ch. Dott of Gorseycop
with her daughter Molly-
blob

(Edward Reeves)

Ch. Jen Kai Ko of Lhakang

(Diane Pearce)

Keytor Midas

(Diane Pearce)

Comte and Comtesse René d'Anjou with their Shih Tzu at Peking Dog show, 1936

(Serge Vargassoff)

General and Mrs. Brownrigg and Miss E. Hutchins *(centre)* with their Shih Tzu at Cheltenham Show, 1933

(Sport and General)

A group at Bath Championship Show, 1973. *L to r*: Mrs. B. Carey and Fishponds Guy Fawkes; Mr. B. H. Halton and Ch. Simone of Sandown; Mr. J. Carter and Montzella's Tsi Chou; Mrs. M. Hoare and Gorseycop Gold Dust; Mrs. D. Harding and Ch. Sarawana Chiu Mei of Taonan

to remove some of the wetness. I use a hair dryer and a fan heater for drying, brushing the coat all the time to separate the hair. Dry the dog all over, not just one part at a time, and be careful not to have the hot air too close. He may not like to feel his face and ears being blown, so dry these well with the towel and brush. As the coat dries, blow the warm air up into it through the hair, which will help to dry it underneath and give it more body.

I use the comb while the coat is still damp, although some people consider this takes out the undercoat. Be quite sure that you dry the dog thoroughly – heat from the body continues to draw out the dampness for some time.

If your dog is being bathed in preparation for the show ring, do not let him dry off by running about in the garden even if the sun is hot – he will rub and rub himself in the effort to get dry, rolling on the grass or somewhere even less desirable. A well-known breeder used to allow her animals to do just this, but her dogs were hardly an example of perfect presentation! The coat should be bathed several days before a show in order to allow it time to settle and get back its bloom, but if it is washed too early it can be very difficult to keep the dog clean until the actual day.

Dry cleaning

Cleaning with dry cleaning powder (obtainable from pet shops) is the favoured method of some kennels for their show dogs; this also helps to remove dirt and surplus grease. The powder should be rubbed well into the coat and left for an hour, then brushed out completely – or, alternatively, brushed into the coat while the dog is being groomed.

A dog can be cleaned with spirit or with a foam shampoo. There are occasions when this is very useful, particularly for small areas of the coat, but it does not create the same effect as with wet bathing. Application of a dry cleaning powder can also be most helpful, as I have mentioned. However, this does not leave the coat with the same bloom as when a wet shampoo is used.

Talcum powder is very useful in grooming a dog whose coat has become matted. If a little powder is put on the hair when the mat is teased out, it will help to keep the hairs separate.

H

8
Selection

SELECTING a Shih Tzu may be for purposes of breeding and showing, or purely as a companion and pet. Whichever the reason, it is important to treat it as a pet and not as a breeding machine. A pet should be chosen to suit not only the environment in which it will live, but also your own personal preference and circumstances. The buyer who wants a companion Shih Tzu, but also hopes to have a litter, should follow the advice given for those who are selecting for breeding.

It is not easy to keep the Shih Tzu in large numbers unless you have plenty of help, and are prepared to devote a great deal of your time to their care.

Large-scale commercialisation of the breed could well be its downfall. Its continuing popularity as a pet will be based on its fascinating character, thorough soundness, and the fact that it is a very natural unspoiled breed, rather than on its length of coat. Should it ever be bred in puppy farms or factories, and confined to kennels away from human contact, it will never develop its full character. Indeed, your love for it is as important as food and drink to its full development, but you will be amply repaid, for it will increase in intelligence, giving you devoted companionship for many many years, not to mention hours of amusement as well.

It is a very worthwhile experience to rear a litter from a Shih Tzu bitch. Normally they are devoted to their puppies, and never tire of them. A litter reared in the house will develop a far greater intelligence and love of people than a kennel-reared litter whose only human contact is at feeding times.

No one who is out at work all day should own a dog, least of all a puppy, unless they are able to take the animal with them. The Shih Tzu loves the car, which should be parked in a suitable shady place if you are leaving him in it – and will regard this as his own property. I know of several Shih Tzu who accompany their owners to work; they sit either in the clinic or the shop, and since their owners are nearby they are perfectly happy. A house-bred animal is very content with his human companions, but it is kinder to have an older animal rather than a young puppy for such a life.

Selection of a puppy as a pet

If you have no intention of breeding or showing, your choice of pup is much wider. Although it is pleasant to have something especially good to look at, money may be your governing factor, and most of the reputable breeders will vary their prices according to estimated show quality. An experienced breeder can recognise the potentially good specimen far better than the pet owner who just breeds an occasional litter for fun, or because he is hoping for some monetary gain. It is true that many of these people seek advice on the quality of their puppies from the owner of the stud dog or the breeder of their bitch, and take great pride in rearing the litter to perfection. On the other hand, I have also known those who buy the cheapest they can find and then sell the whole litter for the top price!

You have an open choice over colour, purely to suit your fancy, but remember that colour breeding is not yet easy in this breed, that colours are mixed up and that birth colours frequently fade. As for sex, do not believe the uninitiated who tell you that a bitch is so much more affectionate than a dog; this may be true of some breeds, but as I have previously said it is not so with the Shih Tzu, and Shih Tzu dogs are extremely affectionate. Another saying is that 'a bitch is not so likely to run off as a dog', but this is more a matter of family traits than sex. Most Shih Tzu make no attempt to run off, and if they do they can be trained to 'sit and stay', so I feel there are no grounds for basing your choice of sex on those reasons.

Size may be an important consideration to you. If you are a country lover who likes going for walks with your dog, you will be well advised not to pick too short a leg; even the small speci-mens will be very active walkers so long as they are not too low to the ground, for every half-inch makes a difference, and there is more height of leg with some strains than others. However, if you live in a flat in a town and take your dog for walks in the park, this point will not worry you.

Character is most important, and by eight weeks of age the puppies are showing their individual characteristics. There may be a 'bully' who has pushed the others out of the way in order to get the best place at the 'milk bar'; there may be a small one which has been pushed out, or another small one which is really sturdy, tough and intelligent, having had to work hard to keep up with the others. One puppy may have been hand reared, or for some reason had more attention from the breeder; this one is likely to be more devoted to people than to dogs, and is often the ideal companion for a lonely owner. Such puppies can become too humanised, however, and be extremely difficult to get into whelp. A puppy should not be shy at this age, but it is sometimes difficult to tell, and a quiet pup may develop when the bully has left the nest. So much will depend on you, the way you rear it and introduce it to new things.

If you do not own a car, and are perhaps an elderly person who has to travel on a bus, then you will need to pick up your dog. Remember that a Shih Tzu is heavy for its size, and a top size specimen of 18 lb is quite a weight to carry – a smaller one would be easier for you. Very often the larger dogs have deeper barks and are more placid; although the Shih Tzu is not a yappy breed, they will nevertheless bark well as guard dogs in the home.

Should you be buying a companion for an older male dog, I would advise a placid-tempered puppy – neither bully nor coward – over the age of sixteen weeks. It is during the period between twelve and sixteen weeks of age that the order of dominance is decided, and this can make a bully or a coward of any dog for life. If the young puppy is submissive to the older dog, the latter is very likely to bully it when it becomes adult, resulting in fighting.

I have set out a few ideas specifically for the pet owner to consider, but those wishing to know more about the detailed points of the breed with regard to puppies should study the section on selection for show and breeding (pages 118 to 122).

Starting a kennel with adult stock

You may have made up your mind what you intend to do, and be ready to go ahead without any further advice, but just in case you haven't yet done so I will try to give you some!

I have already referred to the relative merits of house versus kennel at the beginning of this chapter, and have also condemned commercialisation. Everything depends on your individual circumstances and the amount of space at your disposal.

Commence with bitches, leaving the choice of a stud dog until you have gained more experience and knowledge of the lines and families in the breed. Using other people's dogs for stud purposes at this early stage will give you a much wider choice.

To own a kennel of Shih Tzu is very hard work, for the breed can be quite demanding if it is treated correctly. If you intend to breed as a hobby, and for the improvement of the Shih Tzu (which in my opinion is the only worthwhile way), you will certainly want to keep one of your own puppies, and this will happen not once but several times.

I think it is best to start with perhaps two adults only, with the aim of breeding from a bitch fairly soon; this will enable her to settle into her new home and give you the chance to increase your stock. Keep the other one for show. It is not always so easy to buy adult stock, but if you can afford it some of the top kennels may have young show stock which they will sell, as they like to keep puppies for show and must restrict their numbers.

I must warn you that you will have to be very strong-minded not to end up with more than your original foundation stock!

Several Shih Tzu can live together quite happily and peacefully, unless the presence of one jealous animal causes fighting to start. Some stud dogs can be kept together, but there is likely to be trouble when the bitches come into season, and once fighting has started it may well continue. In such circumstances the only answer is separation or to get rid of one of the trouble-makers altogether, and this can be quite heartbreaking. Shih Tzu can also be very territorially minded, and pounce on an intruder, although a visiting animal will be treated with due respect and courtesy.

Having decided on the number and approximate ages of the animals with which you intend to start your kennel, you must set about choosing your stock. Obviously, those who are already breeders will know what method of breeding they intend to employ, so the following section is written for the newcomer into the world of dog breeding.

If you are planning to build up your own strain, it is advisable to choose stock having a parent or grandparent in common. You need a specimen whose qualities you particularly admire, a dominant one throwing its own type. This is where it is helpful to go round the shows and see the various animals, particularly to the breed club championship shows where you have the opportunity to see the grandparents in the veterans' class, and where the progeny class can also be very informative. It is best that the animals you select should be of a similar type, for in this way you are less likely to breed stock resembling different lines, some taking after one strain in the line and others taking after a different strain. For this reason it is best to have only the one common parent or grandparent, but common antecedents further back are not so important as the influence is not so great. There should be no outstanding faults, only those which can be bred out in one generation. The bitch you choose should, of course, be a very good representative of the breed, though you are unlikely to get perfection, for a breeder thinking that he or she has a perfect bitch would be unlikely to sell her to you unless you are prepared to pay very highly!

You may decide to go in for one or two different colour lines, which is always fascinating, but somewhat complicated in the breed at present. Gold would probably be the easiest, or black and white.

Selecting the stud dog

The same principles apply here as in the chapter on Mating and Whelping. Great care must be taken in selecting a stud dog for your own kennel use. He must suit your bitches, and although a study of pedigrees will be of considerable help one cannot be sure until after the pups are born and grown up. It is far wiser not to buy your own stud dog at first.

Selecting a puppy for show or breeding

First, it should be made quite clear that 'any old throw-out' will not make a good brood bitch. She must be a good representative of her breed, and although she may have some minor faults which you would prefer not to see in a show bitch, these must be ones she is unlikely to throw to her puppies, or can be improved on in one generation. In other words, buy the very best you can. A puppy from a good, even litter is likely to throw better stock than the only good puppy out of a poor litter.

No one can pick with absolute certainty at eight weeks of age, although with your own strain – or another with which your are familiar – it is obviously much easier. Different strains grow at different stages in various ways. Having kept different lines myself I find this is very noticeable, therefore it follows that it is best to go to a breeder who know his own stock rather than to a pet shop or puppy farm.

You may be selecting for yourself from your own first litter, and hoping to retain the pick of the bunch. You will have had every opportunity to study your puppies, and in the course of observing their action you may have found that there is one which catches your eye – maybe because of its flashy colour, or because of that indefinable quality which is so often coupled with a correctly assembled body. A certain amount can be assessed at birth: for example, a good skull nearly always remains good, a very long thin body will stay that way but a short body may grow out.

The longer you can defer making your final choice, the better, but in any case do not come to a final decision before the pups are eight weeks old. At this age you can feel the width of head, and depth of stop. I prefer a high forehead. Although I have known shallow stops deepen as late as six months, these have usually been with the straight nose. The tipped-up nose will give the better expression, and though a Pekey type of puppy head often develops well you do not want too short a nose, and it should be set level with the bottom rim of the eye.

If you want your puppy for breeding or stud purposes, do not choose one which has had nostril trouble as a whelp, as this is likely to be inherited. However, if the nostrils have merely tightened up a little during teething, this is quite a common occurrence and will correct itself by the age of four or five months.

Preferably, there should be no flesh marks between the upper lip and nose. While not a compulsory proviso, and at this age there is still a chance for improvement, the absence of any such improvement can mean that this will look worse as the puppy grows. One which is badly flesh-marked – and sometimes the

upper lip is pink as well – is not so likely to be awarded top
honours, with the present-day high standard in the ring. The
pink tone can become quite vivid, and when the lip is affected
the animal looks as though it has been using lipstick!

A nice round well-spaced eye, showing no white, should be
aimed for. Ideal head markings are a good white top-knot with
white hair between the eyes, and an even white mask – or a plain
black mask in some golds.

The teeth may not all be through, since some puppies cut
these very late and the Shih Tzu is often later than other breeds.
It is better to judge by the gums, which should be broad and
square, and either dead level or with the lower only just outside
the upper, since an undershot jaw tends to worsen as the puppy
grows. In some lines the bite will start by being slightly overshot;
frequently this is perfect by eight to ten weeks, but if it is much
over I would not risk the chance of it correcting. Such puppies
are usually sold more cheaply as pets, and are not suitable for
foundation stock.

Watch for the ear set; long, thick ear leathers are to be preferred
and help to give width to the head. Long furnishings always
disguise short ear leathers in the adult.

The rib cage will alter later, as the puppy bones are very soft,
but the puppy should not be slabsided. If excessively broad, it may
have a roll in front, and while I think considerable care is needed
in the correct rearing of such a youngster, all may be well with the
right care.

Kinks in the tail are likely to stay kinky – but tails are strange,
and I suspect them to have late developing genes; I have known
perfect tails to go kinky well after eight weeks, and these were not
the Swedish tight tails which usually show early. Tails with just
a suspicion of a kink may end up by being perfect. A long tail is
good, provided it is set on high and well held. A tail set too low
will never look good, but remember that the tail is inclined to
slacken during teething.

Some puppies are down in front, some never come up, and
others develop this part late. A front which is constructionally
bowed will not improve, but a loose front should tighten with
care.

One cannot be sure of the length of back at eight weeks, since
some lines grow long after six months. A very short back may

remain that way, in which case you will not get the true breed action. This action is noticeably lacking in too many exhibits, and will spoil the beauty of the breed if allowed to continue unchecked.

The proportions of the leg bones do not appear to alter. The upper and lower bones of the limb are about equal in length, but the pastern bones should be shorter, otherwise the puppy will finish high on the leg. Much can be done to improve muscles and limbs with good rearing.

Most coats should be thick and dense by eight weeks, and a sparse coat is likely to remain so. The coarser coat may thicken later, and the gold coat is very late in maturing.

Note how the puppy walks, although eight weeks is very young and action is not good in some lines at this age.

Having paid due regard to the various points of the breed standard, check for hernias. A small umbilical hernia seldom causes trouble, but a large one will need to be operated upon. Inquinal hernias – felt as a lump in the groin – are fairly rare, and here again an animal which is slightly affected will improve with age, but it is doubtful whether an animal with a bad hernia should be bred from. Some hernias are hereditary, and it is wise to seek your vet's opinion.

If you are choosing for show, I feel it is important to pick a bold temperament. The puppy who drops his tail at every new happening, and does not come forward to strangers, is liable to be shy in the show ring. On the other hand, if this is the puppy which you feel you must keep – possibly because it is the only one in the litter of the sex you require, or is easily the best of the litter – then you can do a great deal to help it. Get it inoculated as early as possible, take it with you everywhere, carry it out into a busy town, never allow it to become frightened, and always encourage it by stroking and calming it with your voice. This will mean really hard work and perseverance, but if you have the pup while it is young enough for all this acclimatisation to be completed before it is sixteen weeks old, you will probably get your reward.

Mismarked puppies with uneven black patches over their eyes do not always throw this trait, but it does seem to be more common now than hitherto, and when it occurs in the pick of the litter it is very disappointing, for the animal is no good for show.

All you can do is buy the best possible, having regard both to the choice available and the amount you can afford. There is, however, one other way to obtain a bitch, and that is on breeding terms. These terms are set out by the bitch's owner, and I have known them to be quite disproportionate to the value of the animal, so you must be sure that you are entirely in agreement right from the start. If you have the conditions set down in writing by the Kennel Club, this can save much unnecessary trouble later on. The most usual terms are to give two puppies to the bitch's owner, a first and third choice. You must appreciate that you will be handing over the pick of the litter, but you may not have the experience and knowledge to recognise the best of the bunch yourself anyway, so it can be a great help to have a knowledgeable person taking an interest in your first litter while you gain valuable experience yourself.

Another point worth enquiring into when buying a bitch is the number of puppies in her own litter, for the size of the litter runs in families. The average is four, and this is a nice number for any bitch to cope with.

I hope I have given you sufficient information to enable you to go ahead with confidence. The more you can learn about the various blood lines, and the more you can observe at the shows, the better – but do be prepared for different judges to hold different opinions.

9

Mating and Whelping

THE Shih Tzu is an easy whelping breed, and has always been so in England. Do not breed from animals who require caesarean sections, but keep the breed natural without any of the gross exaggerations which can lead to deformities. This was Lady Brownrigg's main fear, for she could not bear to see any animal suffer.

It seems a retrograde step to try to breed too closely to the points laid down in the little Chinese book of Madame Lu Zee Yuen Nee. The chapter on disease points out that 'bitches have great difficulty in the delivery of puppies. Because of the long coat, flat mouth and short legs, the bitches cannot lick the organs at the time of delivery, and the bitches are not active in exercise during pregnancy. The weakness of the pups also makes labour difficult, often causing the death of both the pups and the bitch.' This is surely something we should be endeavouring to avoid, rather than breed to. There are other references to the difficulty of breeding the Shih Tzu in the Imperial Palace. I cannot go along with the idea that this was purely due to the eunuchs' inexperience, because they were experienced dog breeders, and the majority of our own early breeders – who had no whelping troubles – were not. Our breeders did, however, suffer considerable loss with the puppies, but veterinary science was not then so advanced in curing diseases. Never let us sacrifice our easy whelping breed for the sake of whims and fancies. I quote from a letter written by Lady Brownrigg to the Kennel Club:

In the years we were in China the dogs we saw were mostly bigger than those we brought home – ours were 12 lb 2 oz, 13 lb 10 oz and 14 lb 9 oz – one of the great virtues of the breed has been their facility in whelping. The only tragedy I had was a very small bitch which we acquired later in China and who died whelping.

It is surprising the number of people, now well-established

breeders, who started off by buying themselves a pet, falling in love with the breed and deciding to go in for showing and breeding. Sad to say, the adorable pet is not always suitable for this purpose, so if you do contemplate breeding from your pet, be sure to seek advice from an experienced breeder as to her suitability. Your bitch must be a true representative of the breed, and should not carry too many faults.

Having ascertained that your bitch is of the necessary quality (for to breed from a poor specimen can very soon help to destroy the breed you love), you must carefully consider all the other snags. It is two months before the puppies arrive, and another two months before they are old enough to leave the home. A great deal of your time will be taken up: you may not be able to sell them to suitable homes straight away, and young growing puppies need space, and time to train, for you will have to give them some training while they are in your charge. By twelve weeks of age they need to be inoculated – it is false economy not to do this. The cost of rearing a litter correctly is considerable, and the bitch requires three times her normal food intake whilst nursing. You will be most fortunate if you do not have to meet any veterinary surgeon's bills, and stud fees are also quite a heavy item. Looking on the black side, you could be unfortunate enough to lose the whole litter after paying out most of the expenses. If the puppies become ill you will have to work night and day looking after them, and suffer heartbreak if they die.

Never breed purely because you have been told that 'one litter will do her good'. One litter will not prevent pyometra later in life, and the safest way to avoid that is to have her spayed. I am afraid breeding does not prevent false pregnancies either, and a bitch who has these is often very difficult to get into whelp.

If you decide to go ahead now, at least I have made you aware of some of the difficulties! The greatest one of all, which I have not yet mentioned, can be having to part with those lovely little balls of fluff. You will have come to love them dearly, and they in return will love and trust you (indeed, if this is not so, then you should not be breeding!). It may not seem difficult now, but I can assure you from experience that it is. I have kept several animals either because I could not bear to part with them, because I thought the prospective buyer unsuitable, or because the puppy did not settle well in its new home and I took it back.

The stud dog

The advisability of keeping your own stud dog is debatable. It is certainly not a good idea to keep a stud dog with the fixed idea that you will never use anyone else's. Neither is it really sensible to commence with one; gain some knowledge and experience first. You may have chosen the dog carefully, but you can never be quite sure what hidden genes he has – nor your bitch either – nor how they will combine with each other. You might be lucky, but then again you might not. Every breeder has a responsibility to work with the sole aim of improving the breed; this is not only true where showing is in mind but is equally important where pets are concerned. It is a matter for regret when breeders disregard anatomical or structural points, and this position – which can be brought about by over-emphasis in judging on the outward stationary appearance of the dog – can eventually lead to disaster.

One should never use 'the dog down the road' purely because it is convenient. Always try to choose the most suitable dog for your bitch, and seek advice from the breed clubs if this is needed. One of their main functions is to give help and advice with the prime objective of doing everything possible to improve the breed.

Do not keep a stud dog in with a bitch unless there are facilities for separating them when she comes into season and you do not intend her to breed. It is also unwise to keep a dog too near an in-season bitch for any length of time, since he could well lose the desire to mate.

In this breed the best age to start training a stud dog is about ten months. A dog who is left after two years often loses all desire to mate, and sometimes has no idea which end is which! Having used him for the first time – not on a maiden bitch but on a placid matron – do not use him again for at least two months. He has not yet reached his maximum development, moreover most stud dogs of quality and keenness are also show dogs, and too much stud work at an early age can ruin their top line, which should be level. Stud work is inclined to make them roach their backs, and – since at that age they are likely to be shedding their puppy coats – the second coat may not come in so well, which could give you a few months with a very short-coated dog.

Always keep your stud dog in top condition, well exercised and well féd. Give him extra protein if he is in frequent use, but do not allow him to become too fat. Diet is important for fertility, and a varied and balanced diet will ensure that he has the necessary vitamins. Yeast tablets or Bemax will provide Vitamin B which is lacking in many diets, and the addition of green vegetables is also a help. On the morning of a mating, it is a good idea to give the dog a raw egg. He should not have a meal before a mating – if he has been fed, and is still able to mate the bitch he is likely to vomit.

As the owner of the stud dog, always ask to see an unknown bitch's pedigree before consenting to use him, because he will be blamed for poor puppies even though he is no more than 50 per cent responsible! It is just possible that the bitch may be cross-bred (this has happened) or that the breeder never gave a pedigree because for some reason or another the bitch was sold 'not for breeding'. No reputable breeder will object to your making such a request.

State the dog's stud fee, remembering that if he is unproved it is usual to give a free service. If he is a good young dog, you will have no difficulty in finding a sound suitable bitch whose owner is willing to accept your offer. You might consider suggesting that a small stud fee should be paid if the mating results in a litter, but you may not have a very wide choice of bitches if you follow this course.

The stud fee is normally payable immediately after the service, and it is paid in consideration of the work done by the dog. If there are no puppies, it is unfortunate but you do not return the fee. Most stud dog owners are just as anxious for the bitch to beget a litter as her owner, and will usually offer a free mating next time with the same dog.

A copy of the dog's pedigree should be handed over to the owner of the bitch on receipt of payment.

It is the responsibility of the stud dog's owner to see that the visiting bitch is carefully looked after. She may have been sent by train, in which case she must be collected immediately on arrival at the station, and given a rest and a drink before being taken to the dog. Before the return journey you should notify the owner of the expected time of arrival, and put the bitch aboard the train yourself – do not leave this to the guard. Should it be necessary for her to stay overnight, then she must be given suitable quarters; many are house pets, and under no circumstances should be pushed outside in a shed on their own. This will terrify them, and they will try to tear a way out. It is not always easy to keep other people's bitches when in season, for they can create a great deal of noise and disturbance, and you must make adequate provision for their accommodation.

Of course, it should go without saying that your stud dog must be clean and free from parasites and all infection.

The service

Two services are advisable if there is any doubt about the correct day, or if the first service was on a maiden bitch who was not relaxed. Provided both parties feel satisfied that the bitch was ready and the mating has been satisfactory, then there is no need for a second attempt. If a second mating is being given for other reasons than the above, then this should be done 24–72 hours later. If there is a tie, the sperm can live for up to 48 hours, and the ova – after they have come down – can survive for the same period.

It is best to use a small room where the dogs, if free, cannot move too far. A table is sometimes used, which does save much crawling around on the floor, and with the long hair of the Shih Tzu it is much easier to see or feel what is happening. Immediately before mating, give the bitch the opportunity to relieve herself.

Never throw a dog and bitch together and leave them to get on with it. The stud dog may get injured, and the bitch may become very frightened and snap at him, the end result being a useless stud dog, a bitch who is always difficult to mate, and no puppies at that. This is just one of the reasons why one should not go to the nearest pet dog down the road. The stud owner has an important part to play in this operation, and if the dog is to be any good at regular stud work he needs help in learning his job.

Whether you use the floor or a table, a non-slippery surface is essential. A table should be steady, and not so big that you cannot hold the animals without stretching right over. Disparity in the heights of the animals may have to be compensated for by placing a pad under one or the other.

If you are completely inexperienced at matings it is advisable to seek the help of an experienced breeder. Things do not always work out as simply as nature intended, and it is best to have an assistant who can help by holding the bitch. Do not have any other spectators, this will only worry the dogs. The assistant – who may be the bitch's owner – must be ready to hold her in front and prevent her snapping. The stud dog owner should be ready to help the dog by seeing that the bitch's tail and trouser hair are not in the way, and to assist in any other way required. Also, some bitches completely collapse on the table, and need to be supported.

The dog will mount the bitch (a smear of Vaseline beforehand will facilitate matters) and once he has penetrated it is most important to see that the bitch does not move suddenly, else he will slip out before the tie is effected. The tie is peculiar to the dog and no other animal. After a few seconds the bulb at the body end of the dog's penis will swell, and at this point a maiden bitch may cry out and try to extract herself from the dog, but she must be held still and calmed. Sometimes the dog does not tie inside the bitch, in which case it is necessary to hold him in position. This is the important time during which the sperm are actually being ejected by the dog, and the first sixty seconds are absolutely vital. A long tie does not necessarily mean a good mating, only that the seminal fluids will help to protect the sperm and enable them to live longer. Should the bitch's ova not descend until the next day, there is more chance of fertilisation than if no tie occurs. The dog, still attached to the bitch, may turn himself, or you can help him to turn so that they are standing tail to tail. You should then keep hold of the tails in case one or other tries to pull away.

After it is all over, the dog will lick himself. Make sure that the sheath of the penis is back in position, if it is not you may have to gently roll it back. Put him on his own for a while – certainly not with another dog or there will be a fight. Take the bitch somewhere where she can be quiet, and do not allow her to pass urine for at least an hour.

Choice of a sire

When choosing the sire for your bitch, do not go immediately for the reigning champion purely because you think you will sell

Jungfältets Jung Ming, 1958

Am. Ch. Golden Talon of Elfann

Aust. Ch. Geltree Cheng Liu

Am. and Can. Ch. Sitsang Whiz Bang

your puppies better and at a higher price. This might be the case, but if he is the wrong dog for your bitch he may not be able to throw his good points to her unless he is a very dominant sire; then if your puppies do not come up to standard, you will have achieved nothing.

It is always a good idea to ask the opinion of your bitch's breeder regarding a possible sire. Recognise the faults in your own animal first, and try to choose a dog who neither carries the same faults himself nor had parents or grandparents with them.

Study the pedigrees, also the dogs at the championship shows, their puppies and the dams of their puppies. Look out for the good points you require in the same way. Choosing with the aid of genetics can always help, but it is still only a partially discovered science and some of the complicated genes are still rather a mystery. It is extremely important to remember that the dog carries many hidden points, and this is where it is useful to know the forebears. Eleanor Frankling's book *The Dog Breeder's Introduction to Genetics* is well worth reading, but I do not propose to go into the subject here.

Having chosen your dog, approach the owner and find out if he is willing to use his dog on your bitch. He will naturally wish to see her pedigree. Tell him when she is due in season, and again when she actually commences, so that it will give him some idea of the day when she will be ready. Also ascertain the cost of the stud fees.

If you have kept a check on the length of the first season, when she stopped showing colour and showed signs of being ready to accept a dog, you should have some indication of the day on which she is most likely to be ready this time.

The season

The age of commencement of season varies from six months to ten months, and I have known it to be both earlier and later than this. Never breed from your bitch too young. The second or third season is best, preferably before she is three years old. Too young a bitch has not completed her own growth, and cannot be expected to put all she should into her puppies while she is still developing herself.

A bitch normally has two seasons a year, but some are awkward

I

and have only one. Others have three, but one of these is usually a 'false' season when no ova comes down and conception cannot take place. She should normally be kept confined during her season, but this does not mean she must be kept in a box. Do not let her run loose on her own, even in your own garden, unless it is secure. If there is no garden available and she has to be taken out for walks, carry her away from your front gate and if possible take her to an open secluded space by car. It is better to let any stray canine Casanova come sniffing at somebody else's front gate rather than your own, for he won't stay there very long if there is no bitch around. It is not only the odour of her discharge which attracts the dogs, but her urine as well. The attraction from the urine commences before she actually comes into season, and you may notice she 'spends more small pennies' than usual. There are preparations on the market which are said to prevent dogs from scenting the in-season bitch, but most of them smell very strongly themselves and can be unpleasant to have around the house. I find veterinary Amplex tablets are excellent, and if you take the precautions I have mentioned you should not have much trouble.

You can tell when the bitch is coming into season, by the swelling of the vulva; she also becomes playful and skittish in her behaviour, even when elderly, and as I said above she passes urine more frequently. It is even possible for a trained house bitch to misbehave by accident on these occasions.

The season comes in three stages and normally lasts for 21 days, sometimes less, frequently more. An abnormally long season in an old bitch may well be the first sign of impending trouble.

Firstly there is a straw-coloured discharge, which in a few days becomes darker and the colour of blood. The vulva is swollen but hard at this time. Then the colour lessens to straw colour again, and the vulva softens, at which stage the bitch is usually ready to accept the dog. Lastly, the vulva then subsides to normal, the discharge gradually decreases, and the bitch will probably be over her season after the third week. She must be kept away from dogs all this time except for the mating; if she is to be mated, do not give her Amplex or any other 'keep-away' preparation. Even after the mating she must still be isolated from other dogs, as it is possible to have a dual conception, in which case the names of both dogs have to go down on the pedigree of the puppies.

Should an accident occur, and the bitch becomes mated by the wrong dog, rather than let her have the unplanned puppies ask your vet to give her an injection to prevent the unwanted conception. This must be given as soon as possible within 48 hours, then her season will recommence and you must be careful to see she does not get mated again.

To summarise, a bitch is ready to be mated when her vulva has softened, she swings her tail sideways and usually when the discharge has become straw-coloured for the second time. A shy maiden bitch seldom swings her tail or flirts with the stud dog, however, and it can then be difficult to be sure of the correct time. Never force a mating on her unless you are quite sure that she is ready. It is ideal when the bitch 'stands' voluntarily for the dog.

There are preparations on the market to postpone the bitch's season, but I do not personally recommend these but have had little experience in their use. In any case you need to consult your veterinary surgeon a month before the bitch is due.

If the stud dog lives some distance away, it is better to take the bitch than to send her, and so long as it is her correct time and you have chosen a proved and experienced stud, you should be able to return with her on the same day. However, if you do have to send the bitch, do so a day in advance in order to give her a chance to settle. Be sure to put her in a very secure box, correctly addressed, to the nearest station where the dog's owner can meet the train. Choose a through train even if it means going to London to put her on it. Far too many animals have been left waiting on a draughty station, hungry and scared.

It is often possible to arrange to give the stud owner a pick of the litter in lieu of paying a stud fee, but this arrangement does have a number of snags. Firstly, any such agreement should always be in writing, thus avoiding argument, for memories cannot be relied on where arrangements are purely verbal. This can be advantageous if you do not want to keep any of the puppies yourself, and another puppy will frequently be bought by the new owner to keep yours company, as two always thrive better than one. A further advantage is that you can save an expensive stud fee, and it is also a good thing if the bitch has been difficult to get into whelp, being one of these four-monthly season bitches. Against all this, the stud fee is often only half the value of a puppy, and if you want to keep one from the litter you will be losing the best before you start. Should you decide to come to such an agreement, then I do suggest that you register the puppy under your own affix, provided that you have one. Otherwise you will not be recognised as the breeder on the pedigrees in subsequent generations.

Always be prepared to leave your bitch for a mating the following day if necessary. You may have the wrong day, or the dog may not oblige. Make sure first that the stud dog owner has sufficient accommodation for your bitch, should it be necessary to leave her.

After the bitch has been mated there are two very important 'don'ts'. *Don't* let your bitch relieve herself for at least an hour. *Don't* let her get with any other dogs, because she is still vulnerable.

The oversexed pet dog

If you have a pet dog who is oversexed, you are sure to be told by well-wishing friends to find him a wife! We will presume he is of good quality and could be used at stud, but it is extremely doubtful whether one mating will satisfy him, rather will it whet his appetite for more. Even if you are perfectly willing to offer him at stud, unless you are known in the breed it is unlikely that you will get many bitches for him. If he is very good, you might try him once to see if he improves; it is possible that his original breeder may like to use him. Should this fail to improve him, I would strongly advise you to seek your vet's advice with regard to having him castrated, which should not alter the rest of his character. An oversexed pet can be a very great trial with children, for it always means that the children's friends, for no fault of their own, get set upon by this sexy little creature. On the whole the Shih Tzu is not this way inclined, and it is only the abnormal dog who can be a real nuisance. For the dog's sake, it is best to remove the urge. Many puppies start this way but very soon grow out of it, and if not used at stud by the age of two they get over it completely.

Whelping. Care of the bitch

During the months before the bitch is to be mated, it is essential that she should receive an adequate mixed and varied diet: mixed, with proteins, biscuit meal and vegetables; varied in its meats, which should contain 4% fat and include beef, mutton, liver, sheep's head, tripe, a little heart, and also eggs, rabbit and chicken. This diet should provide adequate vitamins for general use, but once the bitch is mated extra must be given. This can take the form of 1 teaspoonof cod liver oil and malt or cod liver oil or Vitapet; this last – as well as containing the cod liver oil – has vegetable oils providing Vitamin E. Sterilised bone meal will supply the necessary calcium and phosphorus; give half a teaspoon to each $\frac{1}{4}$ lb of food, also add one teaspoon of Bemax for the Vitamins B and E.

Should you or your bitch object to cod liver oil, there are other preparations on the market which will meet her needs such as St Aubrey's Calcide (Vitamin D with calcium and phosphorus); you must still give the Bemax and Vitamin A, contained in grated carrot. An alternative choice is Crooks Vivomin, which provides all vitamins and minerals in the correct proportions except Vitamin E; the latter should therefore be added, especially since – according to Smythe – this vitamin can be destroyed by the necessary 4% fats.

I give my bitches raspberry leaf tablets: Denes, which can be bought at health shops. These are said to act as a tonic to the uterus and to facilitate whelping. I know for a fact that they have helped my human friends! Administer according to the pre-scribed dosage.

According to Charles Duke, an excellent aid to ensuring black points in the puppies is to give the bitch quarter of a teaspoon of black treacle from the first week after mating, increasing to half a teaspoon before the birth of the puppies, and continuiing with this amount until the puppies are weaned.

Your bitch should be wormed once before she is mated, then again at the fourth week of pregnancy; use a safe vermicide obtainable from your veterinarian. Bear in mind, however, that even this will not ensure that the puppies are free from worms.

Daily exercise is essential from the start in order to keep up the bitch's muscle tone. A flabby, fat bitch is likely to be a bad

WHELPING TABLE

BASED ON 63 DAYS FROM MATING DATE

	1	2	3	4	5	6	7	8	9	10	11	12	13	14	15	16	17	18	19	20	21	22	23	24	25	26	27	28	29	30	31
Mating date JAN	1	2	3	4	5	6	7	8	9	10	11	12	13	14	15	16	17	18	19	20	21	22	23	24	25	26	27	28	29	30	31
Whelping date MAR → APR	5	6	7	8	9	10	11	12	13	14	15	16	17	18	19	20	21	22	23	24	25	26	27	28	29	30	31	1	2	3	4
Mating date FEB	1	2	3	4	5	6	7	8	9	10	11	12	13	14	15	16	17	18	19	20	21	22	23	24	25	26	27	28			
Whelping date APR → MAY	5	6	7	8	9	10	11	12	13	14	15	16	17	18	19	20	21	22	23	24	25	26	27	28	29	30	1	2			
Mating date MAR	1	2	3	4	5	6	7	8	9	10	11	12	13	14	15	16	17	18	19	20	21	22	23	24	25	26	27	28	29	30	31
Whelping date MAY → JUN	3	4	5	6	7	8	9	10	11	12	13	14	15	16	17	18	19	20	21	22	23	24	25	26	27	28	29	30	31	1	2
Mating date APR	1	2	3	4	5	6	7	8	9	10	11	12	13	14	15	16	17	18	19	20	21	22	23	24	25	26	27	28	29	30	
Whelping date JUN → JUL	3	4	5	6	7	8	9	10	11	12	13	14	15	16	17	18	19	20	21	22	23	24	25	26	27	28	29	30	1	2	
Mating date MAY	1	2	3	4	5	6	7	8	9	10	11	12	13	14	15	16	17	18	19	20	21	22	23	24	25	26	27	28	29	30	31
Whelping date JUL → AUG	3	4	5	6	7	8	9	10	11	12	13	14	15	16	17	18	19	20	21	22	23	24	25	26	27	28	29	30	31	1	2
Mating date JUN	1	2	3	4	5	6	7	8	9	10	11	12	13	14	15	16	17	18	19	20	21	22	23	24	25	26	27	28	29	30	
Whelping date AUG → SEP	3	4	5	6	7	8	9	10	11	12	13	14	15	16	17	18	19	20	21	22	23	24	25	26	27	28	29	30	31	1	
Mating date JUL	1	2	3	4	5	6	7	8	9	10	11	12	13	14	15	16	17	18	19	20	21	22	23	24	25	26	27	28	29	30	31
Whelping date SEP → OCT	2	3	4	5	6	7	8	9	10	11	12	13	14	15	16	17	18	19	20	21	22	23	24	25	26	27	28	29	30	1	2
Mating date AUG	1	2	3	4	5	6	7	8	9	10	11	12	13	14	15	16	17	18	19	20	21	22	23	24	25	26	27	28	29	30	31
Whelping date OCT → NOV	3	4	5	6	7	8	9	10	11	12	13	14	15	16	17	18	19	20	21	22	23	24	25	26	27	28	29	30	31	1	2
Mating date SEP	1	2	3	4	5	6	7	8	9	10	11	12	13	14	15	16	17	18	19	20	21	22	23	24	25	26	27	28	29	30	
Whelping date NOV → DEC	3	4	5	6	7	8	9	10	11	12	13	14	15	16	17	18	19	20	21	22	23	24	25	26	27	28	29	30	1	2	
Mating date OCT	1	2	3	4	5	6	7	8	9	10	11	12	13	14	15	16	17	18	19	20	21	22	23	24	25	26	27	28	29	30	31
Whelping date DEC → JAN	3	4	5	6	7	8	9	10	11	12	13	14	15	16	17	18	19	20	21	22	23	24	25	26	27	28	29	30	31	1	2
Mating date NOV	1	2	3	4	5	6	7	8	9	10	11	12	13	14	15	16	17	18	19	20	21	22	23	24	25	26	27	28	29	30	
Whelping date JAN → FEB	3	4	5	6	7	8	9	10	11	12	13	14	15	16	17	18	19	20	21	22	23	24	25	26	27	28	29	30	31	1	
Mating date DEC	1	2	3	4	5	6	7	8	9	10	11	12	13	14	15	16	17	18	19	20	21	22	23	24	25	26	27	28	29	30	31
Whelping date FEB → MAR	2	3	4	5	6	7	8	9	10	11	12	13	14	15	16	17	18	19	20	21	22	23	24	25	26	27	28	1	2	3	4

EXAMPLE: MATED JAN 1ST — WHELPED MARCH 5TH

whelper. The breed has a reputation for easy whelping, and we want to keep it that way. Do not breed for a second time from a bitch who required a caesarean due to an abnormality. Do not breed for excessively large heads or exaggerated short legs; avoid developing the narrow pelvis of the Pekingese.

Towards the end of her pregnancy, as the bitch becomes heavy, allow her to walk at her own pace – do not force exercise on her but allow her a free run. When you pick her up, support her abdomen.

It is difficult to tell whether a bitch is in whelp during the first few weeks. There may be signs such as a change of temperament, she may become matronly or have some sickness during the first week. The teats usually turn a pinker shade. It is not until the third or fourth week that the whelps can be felt by palpating the abdomen. At this stage they feel like tiny pea-like nodules, but it takes an experienced person to feel them and even then it is not possible to be one hundred per cent sure. After the twenty-eighth day these nodules disappear. Some breeders feel it is unwise to have the abdomen palpated at all, and it hardly seems worthwhile if it is done purely to satisfy one's impatience. It is quite normal for a bitch to have a slight colourless mucus discharge during pregnancy. Full gestation period is sixty-three days.

Feeding after 4 weeks

Between the third and fourth week the bitch may go off her food. This is quite normal, and it is far better to let her diet for a few days than to try to force or tempt her to eat. She will then come back to normal with a renewed appetite, and now is the time to start giving her two meals a day instead of one. See that the protein is increased, and that she is having the correct amount of minerals and vitamins. Add an Ovaltine rusk and milk at bedtime to her diet. Always be sure that you leave plenty of water down for her. If she becomes very heavy towards the end of her pregnancy it may be better to feed three small meals, since it is not good for her to overload her stomach. Where a bitch refuses to eat, give half a jar of Brands Essence of Beef twice daily.

Do not let your pregnant bitch run up and down stairs after the fifth week, nor jump off chairs or from any other height. See that she does not become drawn into a fight; other bitches can be very jealous, and may seek a scrap with her if they see you are giving her the extra attention which she now needs. By the sixth week there should be a thickening and hardening of the body at the sides of the abdomen, but sometimes it is still difficult to tell if the bitch is in whelp for she may be carrying one or two of her pups high up under the ribs.

Preparation for whelping

By the fifty-seventh day you should have her whelping box prepared, and if possible try to introduce her to her new quarters.

She will have her own ideas about whelping quarters, which do not as a rule coincide with yours. She may well investigate unsuitable places, such as under the garden shed or in a cupboard, and you must discourage such activities because they usually involve squashing a very fat tummy through a very small hole, and this could harm the unborn puppies.

Choose a place which is removed from other animals, as she will need to be quiet, but equally it should be situated where it is possible for you to have a quick look from time to time to see that all is well. If you must have her in the same room as another animal, see that she has a quiet secluded corner, preferably with a run around the whelping box, so that she knows she is quite safe from prying eyes. A second bitch in the room may try to take over her puppies, and if she objects to this there will be a fight and the puppies will get injured. There are exceptions to this, and some people own wonderfully maternal grandmothers who will foster any puppy, and are always permitted to do so by their grand-daughters.

The whelping box

For the actual whelping I prefer a large wicker basket, kept solely for this purpose. To ensure that it is quite clean, scrub it round with a disinfectant before and after whelpings. I choose a basket of this type because it gives the bitch a rough surface which she can grip and push her back against during the actual whelping. Also the low sides make it far easier to attend to her than if she is in a high-sided box. Line this well with newspapers, to give her material for her bed-making.

After the whelping, when I think she has quite settled down, I put her in the whelping box with her puppies. This should be no smaller than 2 ft square by 18 in high, but if you have a largish bitch then 2 ft 6 in by 2 ft would be much better. My box has a 6-in hinged flap in the front, which keeps the puppies in when they

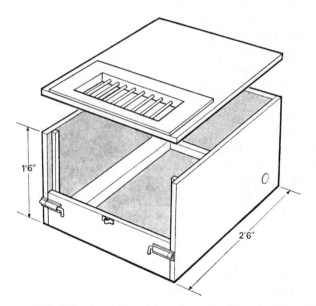

Figure 12 Whelping box. Top hinged at rear. Fitted with retainer to hold in upright position. Front flat with barred window hinged to front edge of lid. Lower front flap hinged at bottom side edges. Safety rails 2 inches from side, 3 inches from floor

are small but can be let down as soon as they get on their feet, for it is then that they like to crawl out of the nest to relieve themselves rather than soil their beds. Above this is a door so that the bitch can be shut in, if necessary. I prefer a door which can be completely removed rather than a hinged one. Do not shut the mother in the box all the time; Shih Tzu are very good mothers, and she will like to get out of the box at times and sit beside it, just watching. There is also a lid to my box, which is hinged.

Inside the box is a rail, placed about 2 in from the sides and 3 in up from the ground. This ensures that the bitch will not lie on her puppies and that her back is not forced against the sides, and also gives the whelps room to wriggle around.

Even if you do not think your bitch is in whelp following a mating, take all the usual precautions. Veterinary surgeons have been known to be wrong, and it is not always possible to be certain. Many a puppy has been lost because a 'singleton' has been well tucked up in the horns of the uterus, and an unsuspecting owner has come downstairs after a good night's sleep to find her poor bitch with one dead puppy.

Once parturition is only about a week away, I make a practice of never leaving my bitches for long periods. I once made the mistake of leaving a bitch five days beforehand; all seemed perfectly well, there were no signs whatever of imminent whelping, she had a normal temperature and was eating her food. Alas, I think the poor thing panicked and brought on her whelping prematurely, for I came home to find three dead puppies tucked under the cushions of the chairs. I learned my lesson then, and pass on my sad experience in the hope that it will save someone else from making the same mistake.

Get your bitch accustomed to her whelping box if you can, and take her up to your bedroom when you go to bed. Not all bitches follow the same pattern, one may show signs 72 hours before whelping and another only 2 hours previously. Though Shih Tzu whelp easily, many have no idea what to do next, especially with a maiden having her first and probably most difficult whelp, who is feeling exhausted. Also, a maiden bitch seldom knows what is required of her until she hears the puppy cry, and if it is in the membranous sac or amnion it cannot cry out. The sac must be removed immediately or the puppy will drown, but there is more about this later in the chapter. With the short muzzle of this breed it can be difficult for the bitch to tear off the sac and bite the cord, and I have known bitches who have injured their pups when doing this.

During gestation there is frequently some colourless sticky discharge which is nothing to worry about. However, if the discharge is yellow, dark in colour or offensive, then consult your veterinary surgeon. It is as well to remove the hair from the bitch's abdomen a few days before whelping is due, since if it is left it will become matted, get in the way of the whelps when they are sucking, and be uncomfortable to the bitch. It can also be a collecting place for dirt and worm ova.

Some people use the temperature test to help them to tell when parturition is due. To do this, the temperature is taken twice daily from the fifty-seventh day; it should be between 100° and 101.4°F. On the sixty-first day an extra reading must be taken at noon in order to register the sudden drop when it begins. The drop will be to around 97°F., and this is when shivering commences, but then it will rise suddenly to as much as 102°F. and at this point the strains usually begin. Personally, I do not like this method, as a matter of routine; it is not good to keep worrying the bitch at this stage.

Remember – always be observant, but don't fuss. See that your whelping tray is ready to hand; on it you will require the following articles, clean, disinfected and sterilised:

Bowl of disinfectant; Dettol or Savlon; soap and nail brush. I like to have a tube of Dettol cream handy as well.

Lint or cotton wool – this is used to grip the puppy if necessary in a breech presentation.

Vaseline – if the whelps get stuck, it is often sufficient just to ease a greased finger round the vulva.

Blunt-ended curved scissors, preferably not too sharp. Blunt ones cause less bleeding.

A pair of artery forceps, to grip and hold the placenta when the cord is cut.

Sterilised thread – this is only required if the cut cord bleeds.

Paper, pen and a timepiece.

Towel, kitchen roll or tissues.

Brandy and smelling salts.

When whelping commences, you will also require to have handy:

Spare newspapers.

A clean box with a banket or towel well wrapped round a warm bottle – don't forget that puppies burn more easily than babies.

Unless you have a warm radiator, have a towel wrapped round

a second bottle, in case you should need to rub down the newborn whelp. The mother may be too busy with one to deal with
the next arrival straight away, and she is also apt to lick them
until they are soaking and then leave them to get cold. If this
happens I take the whelp away, dry it with the warm towel and
pop it into the warm box until the mother is ready.

The temperature in the whelping room should be 70-75 °F.
I do not find that infra-red lamps are a good form of heating for
this breed; they are far too drying, and also unsuitable to put
above the whelping bed, as the bitch gets much too hot. Have a
warm, even temperature in the room, and keep the lid off the box
as much as possible in order to allow the air to circulate. I like to
use a warm pad on a very low temperature in the base of my box.
You can get special canine electric pads, or an ordinary domestic
electric pad can be used. For safety, it should have a soft
mackintosh cover, and be placed underneath a false floor so that
the bitch cannot possibly scratch it up.

Signs of imminent whelping

It is a wise precaution to inform your veterinary surgeon when a
whelping is expected.

Since there is only sufficient space in this book to deal with a
normal and comparatively straightforward whelping, I recommend that more detailed information can be found in *The Mating
and Whelping of Dogs* by Captain R. Portman-Graham.

There are certain signs which indicate the bitch's parturition is
drawing near. She will usually refuse her meal several hours
beforehand, or may vomit it; she becomes anxious and does not
like being left, following you everywhere. Whereas she may have
started to 'bed-make' the night before in a half-hearted fashion, she
will probably begin to do this quite seriously now. Her teats
frequently start filling with milk, though this may not occur until
the puppies begin to suck. After some time in this anxiety state,
which could last all day (and night as well), she may have attacks
of panting. Then she will settle down with her head lying on
her outstretched paws. During all this time she will frequently
ask to go out to relieve herself, but do not let her out un-
accompanied in case she finds a place in which to hide – mine
always try to dig under a shed. Then, lying down quietly waiting,

she will frequently turn her head towards her tail and lick her vulva. Attacks of shivering will occur, the vulva becomes swollen and softens, and there is a clear mucous discharge.

It is most important that you should be with your bitch while she is whelping. She should be in the house, never on any account left to whelp all alone in a kennel; this is not only cruel to her, but you may well end up with some dead puppies.

Although I emphasise that you should be with your bitch, remember that you are there as an observer and to give her encouragement and confidence. On no account must you fuss unduly – if she thinks you can take over, she will probably have inertia.

When labour goes into the second stage, she will give a visible strain, and it is most important that you should make a note of the time when this happens. The strains, which may begin at 15-minute intervals, now become more frequent and more severe, and the bitch presses her rear back against the basket. The first whelp may arrive quite soon, or not for another hour and a half. Do not leave her to strain longer than this. If no puppy has appeared an hour after the start of the first strain, inform your veterinary surgeon; all may be well, but he may not be able to come to you straight away, and no harm is done if the puppy turns up in the meantime. With regard to puppy mortality, according to Smythe the greatest risk in the first born is due to panic on the part of the attendant who tries to effect a delivery before the cervix, vagina and uterus have reached a state of readiness.

The birth

Each puppy is normally born inside a membranous sac, which is attached to the afterbirth or placenta. This sac contains fluid, and the first sign of the birth is usually a bubble appearing from the vulva, followed shortly afterwards by a strong strain when the puppy normally shoots out head first, still in the sac which has cushioned it as it journeyed through the cervix and vagina. Some bitches do tear off the sac and attend to everything themselves, but don't necessarily expect yours to do so, especially if she is a maiden. The short noses of the Shih Tzu also make this task very difficult for them. Remove the sac from the puppy's head first of all, to enable it to breathe, then wipe and clear its air passages. The bitch may want to take over at this point, so allow her to lick the puppy. I am always apprehensive of an excitable bitch who tries to do everything much too quickly. A good bitch licks the puppy all over, and patiently waits for the placenta to come away. Sometimes this comes with the puppy, but if not she will keep on licking; do watch to see if she eats the placenta. As soon as the puppy is free, she will lick it well and thoroughly 'rough-house' it all round the bed—this is quite normal, and is her way of getting the lungs working. Do not rush to cut the cord, for it will certainly bleed if you do. The puppy is coming to no harm attached to the mother, unless of course it needs to be revived, or the mother drags it round the bed, in which case it is likely to get an umbilical hernia, so in these circumstances free the puppy immediately by cutting the cord.

Cutting the cord

Pinch the cord between the thumb and finger of the left hand, about half an inch away from the puppy's abdomen. This procedure is not so easy as it sounds, for if the puppy is short-corded (as are many Shih Tzu) it will be only just outside the bitch's vagina. Having grasped the cord, pinch it tightly to stop the flow of blood; then, using your artery forceps to grip the cord on the other side of your thumb and finger, cut with the curved scissors – pointed downwards between the forceps and your thumb and finger. In this way you will not lose the placenta. There is seldom any bleeding, but if there is, then tie the cord with the sterilised thread. Watch that the bitch does not tear it off again and in so doing shorten the cord too much. You can leave the artery forceps on the end of the cord until the placenta comes away on its own (though you have to be careful that they do not get in the way and stick into the bitch) or, after waiting 15 minutes, you can gently but firmly pull the placenta out. You must wait for a good 15 minutes before doing this, allowing time for the placenta to separate from the bitch, otherwise you may cause a haemorrhage. The retained placenta, if left behind, usually comes away with the next puppy, leaving the second placenta inside.

The next puppy may follow immediately, or not for another 1–3 hours. This varies with different bitches, which is one reason for keeping a record.

If the bitch does not attend to the puppy herself, it is up to you. Whilst it is still attached, rub it over with your warm towel, and if it needs reviving cut it clear of the bitch as mentioned earlier. Hold it downwards to drain the fluid from the nose and mouth, and rub its chest briskly. It should then cry, and you can put it to the bitch to suck or in your warm box.

Resuscitation of the lifeless whelp

Rub the whelp briskly but gently on its back and chest with a warm, rough towel. The rubbing and warmth frequently bring life into the pup, but if this is not effective then hold it head downwards, making sure that the tongue is well forward, to enable any fluid to come away from the air passages. Taking it in both hands, with your thumbs behind its head, swing it forward and down so that its head is swung downwards and then back up again.

Never do a direct mouth-to mouth kiss of life, as the whelp's lungs are far too small and the pressure would be too great. A drop of neat brandy on the tongue, or the use of smelling salts, may make it gasp and start to breathe. Now place it on the warm bottle, and you may have the satisfaction of seeing it revive.

The bitch should now be lying quietly with her head between her paws waiting for the next puppy. The second pup may pop out without even a noticeable strain, particularly if the first has been a long time in coming. The bitch suddenly turns round and commences frantic licking, and by this time she is often well able to attend to most things herself.

When there is a long pause between the puppies, I find the bitch usually likes to have them in with her, and they can then be put to suck, taking each one away again when she shows signs of producing the next in the litter. If she has all her puppies taken from her and can hear them cry she will get very worried, and this prevents her from concentrating on the job in hand. It is best to leave her with one or two, and take away the extra ones. She is not very good at keeping them warm at this stage. If there is a weak puppy, I do not put it to suck directly to the bitch, but keep it in the box on the warm bottle.

As each puppy is born, merely give it a cursory examination, as it will upset the bitch to see you handling her pups more than necessary. When the newspapers become wet, just put fresh ones on top in order to disturb the bitch as little as possible.

I have given a detailed description of what may need to be done, but I must stress as before that your job is to observe without unnecessary fussing. Give confidence by your presence, and occasional encouragement by your voice, doing no more than is necessary; if you are over-anxious you will impart this to the bitch. Many bitches have their puppies so easily that one or two have been born before you realise anything has happened.

Although the Shih Tzu are good whelpers, they have a large number of breech puppies (i.e. born with the legs first instead of the head). The bitch seldom has trouble in delivering such puppies, but if the first one is a large breech it can sometimes become stuck half way, not coming right out after one big strain. In this case, if it is out of the sac you must not delay. Hold the slippery pup firmly with the lint or cotton wool, and on the next strain ease it out. Do not pull on the puppy except when the bitch strains.

I have never had to interfere more than this at any of my whelpings, and it is most unwise to insert your finger into the vagina to see if the head is down. If you are ever in doubt, and suspect trouble, call your veterinary surgeon. Should it be necessary to perform a caesarian, this is far safer if you have not pushed in any infection beforehand.

There is some divergence of opinion as to whether or not the bitch should be allowed to eat her placentas, which are said to stimulate the uterus and sustain her for the next twenty-four hours. They certainly make her bowels very loose, which in the long-coated Shih Tzu can mean washing and drying her trousers, during which time she is fretting to get back to her puppies. I allow my bitches to eat one or two placentas; if too many are eaten, they are usually vomited. The important thing is to note carefully if all the placentas have come away, and if you are at all unsure about this, then do get your veterinary surgeon to examine her. He will give an injection of pituitrin, which will cause the uterus to contract and evacuate its contents. In some bitches the uterus is always slow to contract, in which case the bitch requires an antibiotic as well as pituitrin. It is as well to get your veterinary surgeon to examine the bitch after her whelping in any case, particularly if you are inexperienced.

Once the whelping is completed, the bitch usually settles down contentedly with her puppies. Give her a drink of warm milk and glucose, take her out to relieve herself (unless it is wet or cold in which case allow her to use newspapers), and clean up her bed. I use newspapers for the bed for the first two weeks; the puppies cannot get lost in it, and I think the smooth surface is a help to them when they gyrate around.

If you have not yet weighed your puppies, or examined them for sex and any abnormalities, now is the time to do so. Note any distinguishing markings; if you can distinguish one from another it is so much easier to make sure that each one is sucking, etc. In the case of any obvious abnormalities, ask the veterinary surgeon to put them to sleep when he comes to examine the bitch. It is usual, by the way, for masks and noses to be pink at birth.

Opinions vary as to the most suitable material for the whelping bed. In the Gains Report on 'swimmers', newspaper was frowned upon because of its smooth surface, which was considered to be a contributory cause of the condition known as 'swimming': where the puppy's legs are outstretched sideways, it makes paddling movements and is unable to get up on its feet. Thin-ribbed rubber matting, hessian or corrugated cardboard, are all suggested as better bedding because they give a rough surface on which the puppy can grip. However, I have proved that corrugated cardboard used in the first two weeks does nothing to help a 'swimmer'; when the feet of affected pups get in the corrugations they have more trouble than trying to get around on the newspaper. I keep to newspaper myself until the end of the first two weeks, then put in flannelette on which the puppies can grip at this age. Another advantage of newspaper rather than material is that in my experience my bitches go through a frenzy of bed-making between the seventh and fourteenth days, either in the bed itself or in some other corner of the room where they think the puppies should be! They scatter the whelps in all directions, and finally bury them under the paper, where they are at least safe and warm, whereas if this was material they could become suffocated. The reason for this action on the part of the bitch may be that she considers the puppies can now be left for a time whilst she sits apart from them, therefore she covers them up to keep them warm.

K

When to call in your veterinary surgeon

Do not hesitate to call the veterinary surgeon if:

the first puppy has not arrived an hour after the first strain;
three hours elapse between puppies and nothing happens, but
you feel sure she has not finished whelping (she may have
inertia);
she strains for an hour and subsequent puppies do not arrive;
the puppy is stuck and cannot be passed;
any placentas are retained.

On any of these occasions there may be something amiss, and
it is safer to call your veterinary surgeon – even if the puppy is
born before he arrives – than to have a dead bitch or puppy.

Another reason for calling the veterinary surgeon without
delay is reluctance to settle on the part of the dam after whelping
appears to have been completed, in which case there may be a
dead puppy inside.

Even if none of the above circumstances occur, it is a wise
precaution to ask the veterinary surgeon to examine your bitch
after the whelping anyway, to make sure that all is well.

False pregnancies

These can vary, but the condition usually starts about forty days
after heat ends. The bitch will go through various changes, and
may come into milk, which can be quite copious and is prolonged
through self-sucking. She sometimes collects objects which she
regards as her puppies, and will guard them. The best way to
treat the condition is to give Epsom salts to reduce the milk, and
to exercise the bitch daily, not allowing her to sit around and
mope.

Phantom pregnancies

In this condition the bitch does conceive, but the foetus dies early
and is reabsorbed into the system. The body still goes through
the various changes, however, but when no puppies appear the
bitch returns to normal.

10

Rearing the Litter

The first three weeks

No matter how much of a pet you normally make of your Shih Tzu bitch, it is not you she will now want – her whole attention should be given to her puppies. It is important that you do not interfere too much and distract her attention from the job in hand during these early days, but it is equally important to watch out for anything unusual.

She should have her box placed in a quiet corner, away from all disturbances and draughts, and the room temperature should be between 70° and 75°F. during the first week. It is most important that the puppies are kept warm. I do not like an infra-red lamp myself, since this gives a very drying heat, and with her very thick coat the Shih Tzu bitch can get uncomfortably hot. If you do adopt this method, however, a dull emitter should be suspended overhead and to one side of the bed (not centrally) at a height of 3–4 ft. I prefer the use of an electric pad, as I mentioned earlier, or else a hot-water-bottle which is well covered since a puppy burns more easily even than a baby. There is one danger to guard against with an electric pad, in that a puppy who has crawled or been pushed away from the dam may become too contented; in this case it will not cry or make any attempt to return, and the busy mother's instinct may not be aroused unless she hears its cries. If left for too long it will become weak from lack of food and have difficulty in pushing its way in to suck; even though it appears to suck, it cannot ingest the milk, and if not attended to will fade. Supplement its diet until it has gained strength.

After whelping some bitches do not settle well, but become excited and persist in moving their puppies to a fresh bed. This must be avoided, as the puppies can be injured in transit. If you are using a whelping box it is best to shut the bitch in for a while, but if the mood persists your veterinarian may give her a sedative.

For the first three days and nights you must keep a close watch, but without undue interference. It is important to be sure that the mother knows her job. She may refuse to leave her nest, even for a drink or to relieve herself. A contented and placid bitch and contented puppies usually go hand in hand. A bitch cannot bear to hear her puppies cry, or to have them picked up – it worries her quite as much as it does a human mother.

Make sure that the bitch's milk has come in, and that all the puppies are sucking and developing equally. In a large litter a small pup can easily be pushed out. Sometimes the puppies are unable to get a firm grip on the teats, which may be inverted or very small and so full of milk that they have become hard. The puppy then needs to be held to the teat, and the milk gently squeezed into its mouth until it grips for itself. Put the strong greedy one there first to start off the flow, then let the little weaker one carry on. If the teats are very hard and congested, they may need to be bathed and some of the milk drawn off. Do not let this condition get out of hand, or mastitis will follow.

Keep a weekly weight chart, which is a useful reference and guide to whether the milk is being ingested. A whelp usually doubles its birth weight at one week, and thereafter gains an average of 6 oz weekly. Birth weight seldom bears any direct relation to ultimate weight.

Feeding and care of the dam

Vitamins and calcium should be given from the start. Offer your bitch a drink of warm milk and glucose as soon as she has settled after her puppies are born, and leave water near by where she can reach it easily. It is most important that she should have plenty of fluids. On the first day she may get very hot and pant, in which case a teaspoon of Dinniford's Magnesia may help.

Do not be in too much of a hurry to put the bitch on a meat diet, for this will bring on the milk too quickly. For the first 24 hours give fluids only, about five feeds consisting of plenty of milk. On the second day you can add an egg to the milk, and also give some broth. The feeds on the third day may be thickened; give milk pudding or egg custard, and the broth can be thickened with Farex. A little fish or chicken can be given.

The bitch's temperature should be down to 102°F. by the third day, but if not you should inform the veterinary surgeon. Provided the temperature is down, she can commence a solid diet, which must be adequate and nourishing, and high in protein content. By the third week she should be having two-and-a-half to three times her normal amount, with as much milk and water as she will drink. So long as she is receiving adequate nourishment in quality and quantity, there is less chance of loss of coat. Additional vitamins and calcium are beneficial, grated raw carrot helps the milk situation, and you can continue with half a teaspoon of black treacle to help with the pigment until after the puppies are weaned.

The mother's job is to look after her puppies, yours is to look after the mother, see that all is well and only interfere if necessary.

The bitch should be taken out three times a day to relieve herself. She may not want to leave her puppies, so ensure that they are warm and contented, for she will come running back if she hears them cry. Bitches seldom have their bowels open before the second day, and then they usually pass a very loose stool. After the bitch has been outside, see that she is thoroughly dried before she returns to her puppies. Some people prefer to let her use newspaper, which can be very useful in bad weather, but she badly needs to get a breath of fresh air into her lungs and stretch her limbs. Do not take her for a walk, however, as she may pick up some infection and carry this back to the litter.

After whelping, a bitch has a dark bloodstained discharge which gradually lessens. If it persists after four weeks, or is offensive, brown or green in colour, inform the veterinary surgeon. She should be washed under her tail and around her teats, and the latter should also be inspected daily for any signs of congestion (which can lead to mastitis) or sores. After the first three days you can give her a quick grooming before putting her back with her puppies; she will feel all the better for it, and it will enable you to prevent mats from forming, and remove the head hair which otherwise gets swallowed by the mother when she is cleaning herself.

The mother should keep the puppies clean; she will lick their tummies to stimulate the urine flow, and this licking is also an aid to digestion after feeding. She will also lick the anus to stimulate the bowel's action, and clean up their excreta. You must keep the bed clean, changing it if it gets damp, and make sure that the dam is doing all she should. A blocked anus can cause death.

Dew claws

Removal of these is optional; they may be present on all four feet. The Chinese saying that a dog with five toes on all four feet is a good specimen, and that five toes are lucky, has been the major cause of their retention. These dew claws frequently cause trouble, especially the back ones which grow long and into the pads if neglected. They can also become matted up with hair, and can cause pain if they get caught up in the comb. It is preferable to have them removed when the whelps are three to five days old.

Eyes

The eyes should start to open between ten and fourteen days; when the puppies are kept in the dark, they open sooner than when they are in the light. If the eye is slightly sticky, bathe it with warm weak tea or Optrex. It is possible for the eye to open partially and then close; it can become infected inside, and as there is no outlet for the discharge the eye bulges and is very painful. The whelp wails pitifully, and an antibiotic injection from the veterinary surgeon is needed.

When the eyes first open they are a misty blue, but they will clear and darken later. Keep the puppies away from bright light.

Ears

The ears, which up to now have been sealed, will unseal and the puppy will be able to hear.

Progress

By the third week the puppies start getting up on their legs, and there is frequently one who is more forward than the others.

By the fourth week the tails are up and will be wagged when the puppies recognise you by sight and voice.

Gentle grooming can now start, brushing the coat in both directions with a soft bristle brush. Hold each puppy on your lap and get him used to having his tummy attended to. When the mother stops washing his face, you must wipe round his eyes and mouth daily, and as he gets older follow the instructions in the chapter dealing with the coat.

It is most important that you give the puppies plenty of love from the third week onwards. It is claimed that the vital time for puppies to become really well adjusted to people is between the third and fourteenth weeks of life, and that between the third and seventh week is the best time of all for establishing social contact. Once this has been stabilised, their affection can easily be transferred to others. Those animals which are regularly fondled and groomed during this critical period are reputed to learn faster, show more initiative and be generally brighter and healthier because they are more resistant to stress. It is said that the effect of handling is not only psychological, but that puppies so treated develop heavier adrenal glands – these are the organs which produce cortisone and other protective secretions. A rather lovely story appeared in one of the dog papers about a little boy who, when asked on what he fed his dog, replied 'kisses and cuddles'. He was quite correct; some adults do not realise that there are other 'foods' besides proteins, carbohydrates and fats.

If there is a large litter, the mother may decide at about three weeks that she has had enough of cleaning up her puppies and their bed. This frequently happens as soon as meat is introduced into their diet. You must see that the area around the anus is clean, when the mother ceases her stimulating licking the puppies may have difficulty in passing their motions and thus become constipated. The abdomen will be distended, and the puppy distressed and crying. It may help if you gently massage the stomach, and you can also insert the bulb of a blunt-ended thermo-meter (well greased with Vaseline beforehand) into the anus, but be very careful and do not attempt to force it; then withdraw it, and simulate the mother's licking action round the anus by using a warm swab. One teaspoon of milk of magnesia can also be given.

Now is the time to commence their training. It is instinctive in them not to soil the nest, and they will crawl out if possible, so if you put some newspaper close by they will soon start to use it. You must keep the run scrupulously clean, and give the puppies no chance to start the revolting habit of eating their excreta.

The puppy run should have a non-slip surface – *Never* use sawdust, this can get into the eyes and cause ulcers.

By six weeks of age the puppies need a sufficiently large area to enable them to run around and develop their limbs. They will still spend a large part of the day sleeping. The mother should now be given a bed away from her puppies, so that they do not worry her at all hours.

As soon as the puppies' nails become long and sharp they should be cut with a small pair of scissors, otherwise they can claw at the bitch when feeding and cause her pain.

Give each puppy a pet name at an early stage, which they will recognise and respond to. You may in any case prefer to choose their registration names later on as they develop their characters. Papers for registration are obtainable from the Kennel Club. Learning to come when you use their names is all part of early obedience training, for the Shih Tzu can be very stubborn. If the new owner wishes to give them different names from those you have chosen, suggest adding the new name after the old one until the puppy becomes accustomed to it; then the old name can safely be dropped. Otherwise the good you have done with your early training may be undone.

If you can possibly manage to do so, take the puppies out in the car early; this should prevent car sickness which is most frequently caused by fear.

Lead training

At six weeks this is ideal and well worth the effort, for a puppy who already knows his name and loves to come to you will usually follow well, and once he is used to a soft collar he will walk with little trouble. This training must be carried out with each pup individually, away from all distractions; it may be undertaken in a room indoors, or in the garden in good weather, but not in the street.

Teeth

The Shih Tzu is late in cutting his teeth. Usually the eye teeth appear between the sixth and seventh weeks, and the incisors can be felt in the gums; I have known the latter to come through as late as the twelfth week. Frequently the second teeth are not all through by six months. Hard biscuits such as Bonio are ideal in helping the puppy to cut his teeth; I add Calcidee to the diet.

Supplementary feeding and hand rearing

If the litter is large, supplementary feeding may be necessary in order to relieve the dam and/or to assist any individual puppy who shows signs of underfeeding. On the other hand, unnecessary or premature hand feeding may cause the dam to lose interest.

For the first two days one auxiliary feed may be enough, then give a second. Use the same formula as for hand rearing, and give the supplementary before the puppies are allowed to feed from the dam.

Give these feeds with great care, letting the pup suck out of the tip of the spoon if it is able; in this way it is less likely to choke.

There may come a time when the whole litter has to be hand reared if it is to be saved, because the dam has died or become ill. In these circumstances, the best solution is to get a foster mother if this is at all possible. She should be a bitch whose puppies are around the same age, or who has lost her own puppies – though not of course from any infection. Precautions will have to be taken when transferring these orphans to her. The best way is to remove her from her own brood for a short time while you introduce the new puppies, mingle them with her own and rub them around amongst the others in order to acquire their smell.

I have never experienced the situation of introducing a foster mother who has lost her own puppies to another bitch's litter. However, I think it is best if the bitch is first encouraged to lick the puppies thoroughly rather than straight away putting them to suck, as the bitch will most likely resent this. To get the bitch to lick the puppies, I would smear them over with milky food, or preferably with the bitch's own milk.

If you cannot get a foster mother, you may have to undertake the job yourself. Two people are better than one for this job, for it involves night and day feeding and attention.

Milk formulae

Breeders usually have their own pet formula; it is important not to use too concentrated a strength early on but equally to make it sufficiently rich as the puppy develops. I give several alternative formulae here, for – like babies – not all puppies respond equally well to the same artificial feeding:

a) Lactol, made up according to instructions.
b) Humanised Trufood, Ostermilk or other full cream dried milk powders. Make up according to Olwen Gwynne-Jones in *The Popular Guide to Puppy-Rearing,* i.e. 3 oz water (just off the boil) with 1 oz milk powder.
c) Nutrasol, which is used for rearing lambs, as given by Geoffrey West, M.R.C.V.S., in *About Dogs.*

I have found that curds sometimes form when using Lactol, and personally use half-and-half evaporated milk and water. As the puppy becomes accustomed to this mixture, I gradually add milk, then top of milk, instead of the water. I also add a pinch of glucose. Condensed milk can be used, but in which case omit the glucose. When the puppy progresses, I gradually strengthen the feed with egg yolk and also give a little Brand's essence in alternate feeds. At three weeks the puppy is introduced to meat and the milk feed is thickened.

There are no hard and fast rules regarding the mixtures and amounts in hand-rearing; each puppy must be considered individually, and so much depends on how it is progressing.

Goats' milk is considered the best milk to use, because of its high fat content, but this is seldom available. Bitches' milk is very rich in fat, and it is interesting to compare the fat content of the various milks:

goat	5–6%
bitch	9.7–10.7%
cow	3.8%
dried skimmed	1.8%

If the puppies lose their mother at birth, you must keep them warm and not allow them to become dehydrated (which can happen overnight) or they will die. If you cannot get fluid into them by mouth, then glucose saline may be administered by the veterinary surgeon in the form of a subcutaneous injection.

To feed

Have the puppy on your knee, resting on a warm bottle which is protected by a towel wrapped around it. Use a dropper or tiny plastic bottle (a cat bottle or toy one), and commence by giving glucose water in order to get the puppy accustomed to feeding this way. If he chokes and milk gets into his lungs, it may lead to pneumonia and this is the major cause of mortality in hand-reared puppies. Give a drop at a time, and make sure it is swallowed. In all, feed between half and one teaspoon to start. After feeding you must simulate the bitch's licking by gently massaging round the tummy and openings with cotton wool or towelling which has been dipped in warm water. It is most important to do this until the puppy obliges. Once he has learned to swallow, you can use a milk formula.

Feeding should continue in this way, at two-hourly intervals day and night, for the first week, gradually increasing the quantity and strength of the feed and the time intervals between feeding. At three weeks a little scraped raw meat can be introduced.

Puppies which have been hand-fed from birth will accept you as their mother, and become very humanised; it is often very difficult to get them into whelp later on.

Weaning

The question arises as to whether early or late weaning is best. The fact is that there should be no hard and fast rule, since so much depends on the condition of the dam and the size of her litter. You will have been watching the puppies carefully to see that they are progressing satisfactorily, and supplementing their feeds if necessary. Also watch the dam, to check whether she is showing signs of wear; this is likely if she has a large litter, for it is almost impossible to get her to take sufficient to supply their need plus the extra required for herself. If the litter is small, weaning can very safely be delayed, although it is a wise policy to start puppies lapping at three weeks. I find they do not take to this readily while they are still getting ample from their dam, and about a teaspoon once or twice daily is enough. The puppies are fed in front of the mother, who finishes the last of the milk – of which she seems to approve – and worries no more! Do not add any thickening to the milk, it is the starch which upsets their little stomachs.

When weaning commences the mother should be removed from the puppies for longer intervals each day. Do not take her away altogether, because she loves her puppies, and will play with them and teach them to fend for themselves. Between four and five weeks, as they are getting on to solid food, the mother frequently disgorges her own food for them. This is a normal reflex action, but make sure that it is suitable food for the puppies.

There is seldom trouble over the Shih Tzu bitch's figure returning to normal, although she frequently loses all her coat.

At four or five weeks, begin to give small quantities of scraped lean raw meat twice daily, increasing to one teaspoon in two days. Continue with the milk twice a day also. Increase the amount of meat slowly, and by six weeks 2 oz can be given; it may now be minced and should not be fatty. Farex may be used to thicken the milk once the puppies are accustomed to meat. If the puppies do not lap this up at first, let them lick it from your fingers or pop it into their mouths. Eating is a habit, and if they eat well now they should continue to do so.

Specimen Diet at Eight Weeks

8 a.m.   About 2 oz Farex and milk; more can be given, but milk sometimes causes looseness.
Midday   2 oz lean minced raw meat, or an adequate substitute.
4 p.m.   As at 8 a.m.
8 p.m.   As at midday.
A drink of milk may be given last thing at night.

Feed the puppies in individual dishes, and leave water for them to drink at all times. Add vitamins and minerals to their diet – Vivomin by Crookes is a balanced supplement. Eggs, rabbit and chicken may now be gradually introduced. Grated carrot is excellent, and you should continue with half a teaspoon of black treacle or elderberry if the pigment is bad. If a combined vitamin additive is not being given, then add three drops of Adexolin, a teaspoon of Bemax, and a pinch of seaweed powder which is strong in iodine and good for the coat. Garlic, which can be bought in tablet form, is an excellent internal disinfectant.

A puppy should receive 18–25% protein in his diet. Add any extras gradually; it will put him off his food if you introduce them all at once. At twelve weeks you can decrease the number of meals to three, dropping one of the milk feeds. By six months two meals only need be given; I continue with two until at least ten months old.

The puppy will soon tire of Farex and a suitable biscuit meal may replace it; this should be well soaked and added to the meat meal. Saval No. 1 is a good one with which to start. The food should consist of 50/50 meat and other foods, including chopped vegetables, and by six months the amount of meat should have been increased to 6–8 oz, according to the size of your Shih Tzu.

If there is persistent looseness of the bowels, it could mean that insufficient carbohydrates are being given or eaten. A little additional bran or Allbran will remedy this by making extra bulk.

Variations in puppy weights can be considerable, but as a rough guide I find that at about four months the puppy has reached half his adult weight. Between 5 and 8 lb is ideal. At approximately six months, the puppy is usually about two-thirds of his adult weight, and at this point $7\frac{1}{2}$–12 lb is ideal.

At no time should a puppy be underfed in order to keep the weight down. Good feeding is essential to ultimate development and soundness.

Modern feeding conditions

There is a growing tendency to feed dried complete foods, but it is important to use one which has been well tested over the years. Some manufacturers have their own research centres.

If you do use one of these foods, be sure that you do so strictly according to the manufacturer's instructions. You will not have good results if you upset the balance of the diet by adding your own extras.

Worming

Even when the bitch is wormed before whelping, the puppy can still be troubled by worms, usually roundworms. The worm ova can be passed from the dam, via the placenta, before the puppy is born.

Signs of worms in a puppy are a variable appetite, and pot-bellied appearance particularly after meals. There may possibly be runny eyes and a cough, and a generally unthrifty look. Worms can be passed in the faeces or vomited. The vermicide must be obtained from your veterinarian. Present-day vermicides are perfectly safe, and no starving or purging is necessary.

Even when no signs of worms are present – and a few may do the pup no harm – it is the responsibility of the breeder to make sure that worming is completed before the pups go to their new homes. Puppies can pass worms to small children who allow them to lick their faces, or who put a puppy's toy into their mouth. If worms should get behind the eye, blindness may ensue, and while this is very rare indeed, don't let it happen through any neglect on your part. My veterinary surgeon advises routine worming at three, four and five weeks to prevent worms becoming estab-lished. At two-and-a-half weeks the worm comes into the gut as an adult, having spent its previous existence in the larva state in the liver and lungs. If there are no worms present at five weeks, no further worming is necessary until five months. However, if they are still present at five weeks, worming should be carried out again at eight weeks old.

Troubles in the nest

Fading puppy syndrome

This strikes in the early days, when the litter is strong and apparently thriving well. One puppy stops sucking and starts to wail, a plaintive sound which has been described as similar to the cry of a seagull. There are different types of 'fading', possibly due to different bacteria which strike at various ages, each of different duration. As soon as you suspect the presence of 'fading', remove the affected puppy to a warm box on its own, and inform your veterinary surgeon who will give it (and possibly the whole litter) the correct antibiotic injection. This puppy will need to be hand-fed to survive, and frequently several others in a litter become affected. Fortunately, I have found this 'fading' to be rare in Shih Tzu.

Chilling

This is a very great danger for a tiny puppy who becomes parted from the warmth of the dam. Its body temperature falls very rapidly in a cold room, and even when the surrounding air of the room is 70°F. the temperature drop will still occur. It is possible that the dam has discarded this puppy because it has a congenital defect; all puppies who are ill have a 'sick smell' to the bitch. The symptoms may be similar to those of a fading puppy, or it may just lie still and feel limp and cold to your touch. A healthy puppy will immediately go to the teat on being awakened, and grip hard, but one affected by chilling will appear to suck if put to the mother while not actually having the strength to do so. The condition of internal chilling can go on unobserved whilst the puppy becomes weaker. The rectal temperature may drop to 70°F. Two hours spent away from the warm is long enough to cause chilling to start.

As soon as this condition is discovered, keep the pup warm, and very carefully give it a few drops of brandy and water in equal parts. If this appears to revive it, it can be fed about one teaspoon of glucose water. As the puppy may be too weak to swallow, it is safer to commence with water rather than milk. Once accustomed to swallowing the glucose water, one of the puppy-rearing formulas can be fed hourly.

The whelp should return to the dam as soon as it is strong enough to suckle, usually within 24–48 hours. If necessary, express milk from the dam first, and hold the puppy to a good flowing teat. A close watch should be kept in case of a possible relapse.

Nostril Trouble

This condition attacks at ten to twenty-one days of age. Some puppies are born with a tight nostril; this is curved inwards, with a very tiny opening, and is undesirable, but not the condition to which I am referring. Other puppies frequently have wide nostrils at birth, and these do not tighten until the trouble starts.

The cause is uncertain, but is sometimes hereditary. It can be an infection, possibly due to a blow, or because of a variable growth rate in the puppy. It has apparently changed its aetiology, for whereas in the early days penicillin was a cure, it does not now respond to this or indeed to any other antibiotic. At the same time it is a wise precaution to try one.

Symptoms are similar to those of the fading puppy. The pup crawls around the bed, refusing to suck even when in the proximity of the teats. Its mucous membranes are swollen, and it cannot smell. At the next stage it cannot breathe through its nose, it wails continuously with its head up and mouth open, and if left it will eventually become weaker and die.

It is important to notice the symptoms early. The puppy must be hand-fed, and frequently put back to the bitch to see if it will suck; occasionally it will do so, but then relapses. It must, of course, be kept warm. Hand-feed small quantities of a puppy-rearing formula hourly, adding a teaspoon of brandy to one teacup of feed. The duration of this condition is from one to about fourteen days.

Early Deaths

Many an early death goes undiagnosed. There may be internal imperfections; some whelps are without orifices, and these may live for only three days.

Where there is a *hare lip,* an affected puppy is unable to suck, and if this condition is accompanied by a *cleft palate* (which I have never seen in the Shih Tzu) the food is regurgitated. Such puppies should be put down immediately.

In cases of *drowning,* some puppies' lungs do not expand properly, their exit from the bitch may have been delayed, and the puppy drowns in the fluid surrounding it.

The Flat Puppy or Swimmer

I am personally uncertain whether this is one or two separate conditions. The 'flat puppy syndrome' is frequently referred to as a severe condition of the 'swimmer' I have been unable to obtain a copy of a paper written on the flat puppy by Ball and Asquith, and although I have read many accounts of 'swimmers' I have never experienced this myself. I have, however, had a flat puppy, which is shown among the photographs. Her chest was completely flattened at birth, but her legs only straddled as a result of this – there was none of the muscle weakness which is normally found in the 'swimmer', who collapses when trying to stand on its legs without support. From two weeks of age my puppy's chest was gently moulded, until by the age of four weeks she was able to stand (rather widely) and by seven-and-a-half weeks her legs and chest were normal. This rare condition is known in heavy-boned short-legged breeds; it is very rare in the Shih Tzu and from various accounts does not appear to be thrown.

I have read of 'swimmers' being cured with injections of vitamin E. Smythe reports the condition as appearing to correspond to the haemolytic disease of newborn pups, caused when A-positive pups ingest antibodies from an immunised A-negative dam (Burns and Fraser).

Viral hepatitis

Various infections can be transmitted through the dam or sire to the unborn puppies. One dread disease which will attack the strongest and healthiest in the litter is viral hepatitis, an abominable complaint which takes many forms and can kill in a matter of hours. The puppy may pass blood, the veterinarian must be called immediately, and at least inject in order to save the remainder of the litter.

Proplapse rectum

This can affect puppies who have suffered with constipation. The protruding rectum should be gently pushed back inside with a Vaselined finger. Olive oil or liquid paraffin should be given to the puppy to prevent a reoccurrence.

Puppy rash

This may be a milk or urine rash on the tummy. It can be treated with castor oil and zinc ointment, and will soon clear.

Calcium drainage or eclampsia

This is a condition in which the bitch can die within a few hours unless an injection of calcium gluconate is administered, the

L

results of which are immediately effective. Puppies must be taken off the bitch for at least 24 hours, and if returned she must be watched in case a relapse occurs.

The signs are restlessness, excitability and panting, followed by a stiffening of the legs. The temperature rises rapidly to 107°F. or more. The symptoms rapidly worsen, there is profuse salivation, the mucous membranes become dark and congested, the pulse is rapid and hard. If left untreated, tetany sets in and the bitch dies. Send for veterinary assistance immediately the symptoms are noticed.

All too soon the time comes to part with your puppies. Do not condemn them to an unhappy life by selling unwisely. The Shih Tzu should not become a purely commercial proposition, and it will not thrive in an unsuitable environment. Do not sell whole litters indiscriminately for the sake of profit – money does not ensure a good home.

Never sell under eight weeks, for up to at least seven weeks the puppies should still have some contact with their dam. The best age is eight to twelve weeks, but they should not be exported under twelve weeks of age. Do not neglect to have a puppy inoculated (see Chapter 6). Always provide a diet sheet with each puppy, together with further advice on feeding and grooming. Suggest that the new owner joins a breed club – in this way they will be able to contact other owners and more knowledgeable people who are always ready to give help and advice if required.

Although I have given as much information as space allows, particularly appertaining to the Shih Tzu, I do strongly advise new breeders to gain further general information from two excellent books: *The Breeding and Rearing of Dogs* by R. H. Smythe, and *The Popular Guide to Puppy-Rearing* by Olwen Gwynne-Jones.

11

Showing

SHOWING can be a fascinating hobby, so long as one retains a sense of humour and can take the good with the bad. It is also an opportunity to make many friends.

There is little monetary reward to be gained, and considerable expense is involved on entry fees and travelling. Therefore it is important that you should enjoy the day's outing even when your dog is not among the winners.

Competition is keen, the standard is high, and it can be hard work to bring a dog to top show condition.

Some dogs do not enjoy showing, and it is unkind to keep them in the ring. Pet dogs have been known to go 'lame' as soon as preparations commence – this is the Shih Tzu way of informing you that he is not going to play this game!

There are many different kinds of shows. The smallest show, which is a good preliminary training ground for both you and your dog since it eliminates the big winners, is the best one for a start.

TYPES OF SHOW

Sanction

This is the smallest show and is unbenched. Only dogs who have not won five or more prizes of £1 or over in post-graduate or higher classes are eligible. Many big breeders show their young stock at these shows, which ensures that there will be good competition. To enter, you must be a member of the society running the show, but your membership application will usually be accepted at the same time as your entry form.

Limited show

This is also limited to members of the society concerned, and to dogs who have not won any challenge certificates towards becoming a champion. The prize money and entry fees are lower than at bigger shows. It is unbenched.

Open show

All dogs registered at the Kennel Club are eligible for entry to open show, including champions. The larger open shows are benched, i.e. you are given a number for your dog which can be written on your entry card, and will correspond with the number on the bench allotted to you; the dog must be attached to this bench with a special benching chain or lead.

If classes are not scheduled for your breed, there will be non-classified and variety classes for which you can enter.

Championship shows

These are the most important of all, and are the only shows where Kennel Club Challenge Certificates are on offer. Most championship shows now schedule classes for Shih Tzu.

There are now twenty-five championship shows which are permitted to offer challenge certificates for the breed. Two certificates are given, one for the best dog and one for the best bitch. Championship shows have the best classification and the largest number of entries. Entry fees are high, and prize money is low, a state of affairs which has not been changed since at least 1933! Some countries award no prize money at all. Since writing this, an increase in entry fees has been brought about.

Exemption shows

These are frequently held in aid of charities, and are very popular, but show dogs should not enter them unless they are run under Kennel Club rules. There are invariably classes for mongrels and dogs who are not registered at the Kennel Club.

Four classes are permitted for registered dogs. These attract large entries, and winning show dogs frequently come, as naturally with charitable aims in mind the object is to make as much money as possible. They can be great fun, entries need not be made until the day of the show, and there is a generally happy and carefree atmosphere.

One of the weekly dog papers (*Dog World* or *Our Dogs*) will give you all the information you need regarding forthcoming shows, together with the secretary's address, so that you can send for a schedule, but remember that your puppy must be at least six months of age and registered in your name with the Kennel Club.

You now have your schedule and entry form, and are wondering which classes to enter. For a first show it is unwise to enter more than two classes, for your puppy may be nervous and his first show should be a pleasure. If he is under nine months old, and there is a special puppy class available, then this is the best for him, for they will all be young and a very young puppy is not expected to show like a veteran.

I would advise you to give the junior class a miss, since very experienced dogs can enter this one. The maiden and novice classes are the next best to enter. If there are no breed classes scheduled, you can enter the non-classified variety class which will be smaller than the 'Any Variety'. Your schedule will give you the qualifications for the various classes.

If your dog has not been registered with the Kennel Club or transferred from the previous owner, this must be done before the last date of entry to the show. Write to or telephone the Kennel Club at 1 Clarges Street, Piccadilly, London W1Y 8AB, obtain the required registration or transfer form and fill it in immediately. Strictly speaking, you should have had this form given to you and signed by the previous owner or breeder when you purchased your puppy. When completing the entry form, add the letters N.A.F. (name applied for) or T.A.F. (transfer applied for), whichever is applicable. Send off the entry form before the closing date, and if you have not already done so now is the time to proceed with training your dog.

Training

If you have followed the suggestions in my chapter on training, your dog will be walking well on the lead and will have learned to obey you. Ring training is only a short step from this. Many canine societies hold ringcraft classes, and it is well worth attending these if this is practicable. You will enter the ring with a great deal more confidence, and this confidence will be transmitted to your dog at the other end of the lead.

Ring procedure

When your class is called, enter the ring and give your bench number to the steward, who will then give you a card to pin on to your jacket. Then line up with the other dogs and owners, but position yourself down the line if you can so as to have the opportunity to watch procedure.

Talking to the judge is not permitted in the ring, unless you are spoken to first. If you have any queries, address these to the steward.

The judge may ask for the dogs to be walked round. You will then follow each other in a large circle, so be sure to keep your dog on the inner side. After this, each dog is judged separately, first being placed in a standing position on the table where it will be examined by hand for various anatomical points. The head will be felt, the eyes inspected and the mouth opened. If the puppy has not been trained to expect this, he may resist, and if he is frightened and upset it could well cause him to dislike showing. (Grooming on the table at home is a good start to training, and if you have a few friends who are willing to help by handling him lightly at this time, it will not come as an alarming experience at his first show.) His age may be asked, and you will be asked to 'walk your dog' while the judge watches the hind and fore action which is so important in the Shih Tzu. Training here will help considerably, both for you and the dog; if you walk sloppily, so will he! He needs to walk smartly with his head and tail held up. If the judge is watching side action, remember to keep the dog between you and the judge.

After all the dogs have been examined and walked, they are lined up again and the judge makes his final choice. It is important that your dog remains in the standing position at this point in proceedings, after which the winning dogs will be called out to the centre of the ring. In a very large class, a first unplaced selection may be announced, and a final choice made from these.

A few words of advice may be timely here. As I said before, it is not sufficient to have a basically good dog, but if you do have a good one then it is up to you to learn how to make the most of it in coat, presentation, training and ringcraft. Other breeders are usually most helpful to novices, unless the latter seem to think they know it all!

Do not make the mistake of asking too many people for their opinion of your dog. They will all tell you willingly, but you will be very confused by possibly contradictory comments, and the dog's faults will be pointed out to you to such an extent that you will wonder if there is anything right about him at all. You will soon find out the most knowledgeable breeders, but unfortunately even they do not always agree about the quality of each other's dogs. The judge at a show is usually willing to give an opinion if approached after the judging is completed.

If you are fortunate enough to win at your first show, do not imagine that you will win every time. Not all judges come to the same conclusions, and what is important to one may be unimportant to another. If you do not win, the experience will still be valuable, and you will probably learn far more in your efforts to ascertain just *why* you were not successful; this may even be obvious to you straight away, and will help you to avoid becoming 'kennel blind'.

Preparation for the show

Besides the necessary training for the ring, you will want to ensure that your dog's coat is at its best. Each exhibitor has his or her special technique, and here again you may get very confused if you ask too many people exactly what you should do, for the advice is bound to be conflicting. If I pass on some general hints, you can decide what best suits you and your dog.

Before the show your dog can have either a wet or a dry bath. If a wet bath is given, this should be done about four to seven days previously; a dry cleaning powder may be used the day before. Instructions on bathing are given in Chapter 7, Care of the Coat. The reason for bathing early is to enable the coat to regain some of its natural 'body'; if you leave this until the day before the show, the coat will only hang limply. After bathing you must keep him clean – this is not so easy! Daily grooming is essential, because the coat will mat up and tangle more easily after the bath, but be careful not to groom out all the undercoat.

Remember to keep the nails clipped, since long nails have an adverse effect on the dog's action. Clean the teeth with a swab wrapped round an orange stick or your finger, using 'Showite' toothpaste marketed by Crookes.

Equipment for the show

Take with you a bag containing the following:

Benching rug.

Benching chain and collar.

Show lead and collar. Accustom your dog to this before taking him to a show. Never use a harness.

Cotton wool and water or Optrex to wipe the eyes.

Drinking bowl and water – although water is always available at a show, it is not always convenient to fetch it.

Some small titbits, such as liver or sausage. I do not feed my dogs at a show, but let them have a light meal in comfort later on, which they are better able to digest when they can relax.

Your usual grooming tools.

Additional cleaning powder.

A towel, remembering that even if you carry your spotlessly clean dog from the car park, he must be permitted to relieve himself after an early start and a long journey, and may get wet.

Clip or pin to hold your ring number.

DO NOT FORGET TO TAKE YOUR TICKETS.

Many people take their own portable grooming table, which is usually in the form of a small folding card table.

Most championship shows give prior notice as to which dogs are first in the ring, and as a rule this is announced in the dog papers a week beforehand.

Always arrive in good time; an hour before judging is due to start is not too early. You may have a long walk from the car park, and then some trouble in finding your bench. It will not help your dog if you become flustered and rush him into the ring ungroomed. Buy a catalogue, settle your dog on his bench, ascertain (if you do not already know) when you may expect to be in the ring, and prepare to have your dog groomed for that time. There is always last-minute grooming to be attended to with a Shih Tzu.

Preparation at the show

The extent of this final preparation will depend on how much you have done beforehand, and on your mode of travel. If you travelled by train, and your dog was unboxed, he is unlikely to arrive in the immaculate condition in which he left. This is where your cleaning powder is needed, and after rubbing the powder well into his dirty coat you must be particular about brushing it all out again. Even if he has remained clean, he will still require another groom before actually entering the ring. The better the presentation, the greater are his chances of winning. A dog whose thick undercoat is matted will not look so good, even though the guard hairs are long and well groomed, for the body line will be spoiled and he may even look out of proportion. Groom the head and re-tie the top-knot, being careful not to pull in the hair too tightly above the eyes, which would not only be uncomfortable but also alter the expression. Comb the whiskers neatly, putting a little powder on them, but be careful not to get it in the eyes for this will hurt. Wipe round the eyes with a damp swab, or a dry one if time is short; the whiskers must be dry by judging time. Give a final powdering to the white paws, and comb them out, paying particular attention to the inside of the legs which is often forgotten. Check that the trousers are clean and well combed down; if they are bunchy and sticking out you will be adding an inch to your dog's length, and his legs will look too far under his body. All these small details are of the greatest importance and will be learned by experience.

Put the show collar and lead on your dog, remember the pin for attaching your number, and you are all ready for your class. You are allowed to take a brush or comb into the ring with you.

If you do not win, take a good look at the dogs who are successful, and learn all you can about handling and presentation. This will get you a lot further at the next show than joining the ranks of the grumblers. There is always another time, with a different judge. Good luck to you!

KENNEL CLUB TITLES

Junior Warrant

A dog up to eighteen months old is eligible to win this title, to qualify for which twenty-five points have to be gained. They are awarded as follows:

One point for a first in a breed class at an open show.
Three points for a first at a championship show.

One normally expects a junior warrant holder to be of such quality that he will later gain his title of champion, but it does not always work out that way. A Shih Tzu can look wonderful at ten months, but as it is a late maturing dog it does not always retain its good looks.

Champion

It is harder for a dog to gain its title in England than in other countries, for the systems are quite different. In England a dog gains the title of champion by winning three challenge certificates under three different judges, one of which must be gained after the dog is over twelve months old. Challenge certificates are only on offer at championship shows, and then only when the Kennel Club permits. There are still some championship shows which do not have C.C.s for the breed.

There is no limit to the number of C.C.s a dog or bitch may win, and it may also be shown under a judge who has previously awarded it a C.C. Most exhibitors feel strongly about this, however, and generally refrain from entering their dog again under the same judge unless the show is Crufts.

In order to gain a C.C. it may be necessary to beat a formidable array of champions, for they are all entered in the open class. Many excellent animals are unable to gain their title, and I have included pictures of some of them in this book, for it is not always the 'red-lettered champions' in the pedigree who throw the good stock, and information regarding the other dogs is only too often hard to come by.

12

Ailments

THE Shih Tzu is by nature a very robust little dog, and illness and disease do not come his way as often as in some small breeds, although weaklings can be found in any variety. The weakling will pick up infection easily, and the best way to guard against this is to rear your dog carefully and keep him in a healthy condition.

Inoculations against hard pad and distemper, canine virus hepatitis and leptrospiral jaundice are essential. These diseases can be killers. There are different vaccines on the market, and your veterinarian may have a preference. Vaccination should not be done before either nine or twelve weeks, depending on the vaccine used and/or your veterinary surgeon's advice. The puppy must not go out and about before his vaccinations, for if he has already picked up some infection the vaccine can have an adverse effect. Neither should he be out until fourteen days after the last injection; this allows time to build up some immunity.

Correct feeding

This means a well-balanced diet, of sufficient quantity and quality. The over-indulged house pet, who has become fat through eating too many titbits, will most certainly be unhealthy internally. In addition, trouble can be caused by too many vitamins or too much calcium, as well as through deficiencies.

Cleanliness

Kennels must be kept thoroughly clean, and free from any parasites, but do not overdo the disinfectant which should always be measured correctly into the bucket of water. A fresh water supply should be given daily, and all bowls washed out.

A constitutionally healthy dog has a greater resistance to disease, and is able to overcome illnesses more quickly. If a dog is off colour, he will become lifeless and lose the brightness of his eyes (although in fever the eyes become unnaturally bright), and his coat will be dull as is human hair during illness.

If there are more visible signs such as discharging eyes, diarrhoea or vomiting, have him seen by your vet at once. Many infections can start in this way.

To take a dog's temperature, which should normally be 101°F. The temperature should be taken rectally, therefore you will need to keep a special short-bulbed thermometer for the purpose. Shake the mercury down to around 97°F. and insert the bulb end about an inch into the dog's rectum (just below the tail), leave it there for one minute, and if the dog is restless ask someone to help in holding him still. After reading, wipe the thermometer with a swab of cotton wool soaked in disinfectant, then wash it and shake the mercury down again.

Nursing a dog

Keep it warm and away from draughts. Always have water available near by, and offer this to the dog frequently.

This book cannot deal with disease and illness in great detail. It is as well to have a book to which you can refer, and I would suggest *First-Aid and Nursing for your Dog* by F. Andrew Edgson, M.R.C.V.S., and Olwen Gwynne-Jones.

Illness of the whelp have been specifically dealt with in Chapters 6 and 10, of the lactating bitch in Chapter 10 and of old age in Chapter 6.

MINOR AILMENTS

Anal glands

The dog has two anal sacs, one on either side of the anus. These sometimes become clogged, and the dog will then nibble at his tail and scoot across the ground on his hindquarters. The glands will require emptying in order to prevent an abscess from forming. To empty the anal sac, the tail is held up with one hand while, with a large wad of cotton wool held over the opening, you use the thumb and finger of the other hand to gently squeeze from

behind the anus, outwards. It is questionable whether this should
be routine treatment, since it can break down the surrounding
tissues, and is best carried out by the veterinarian. This is also
discussed in Chapter 7.

Constipation

It is unusual for a dog who is on a well-balanced diet to suffer
from constipation, but it can happen, especially if he has had a
bone to chew. If he is straining hard without any effect, make sure
there is not a small sharp chop bone lodged just inside. It sometimes happens that the cat steals a bone and drops it where the
dog can pick it up. Straining can also follow diarrhoea. For treatment, give a dessertspoon of medicinal paraffin, a meat meal
without biscuit, and follow this with a walk. If the dog still
does not have his bowels open, he may need an enema.

Coprophagy

This is an unpleasant habit rather than an ailment, in which a dog
eats his own excreta or that of others. It is quite common in many
breeds, and has been dealt with in Chapter 5 but I will also deal
with it briefly here. This condition is thought to be due to a
deficiency of minerals or vitamins, which are being sought by the
dog in the proteins thrown out in the faeces. It has been suggested
that the addition of a little more fat to the diet would help, by
slowing down the progress of the food through the digestive
tract and thus giving the proteins a better chance to become
digested; fewer proteins then being discarded, the temptation
would thus be removed. Another remedy is a little black treacle
or molasses on the food.

Diarrhoea

This can be very serious, especially when coupled with vomiting,
and must not be neglected as it can herald the onset of various ills.
It is surprising how quickly a dog can lose condition with
diarrhoea. However, looseness of the bowels may be dietary, or
just due to some small upset. Garlic tablets act as a good internal
disinfectant, and a little bran or Allbran with the meat meal

absorbs the moisture and prevents excreta from sticking to the trousers. Some dogs do not eat enough biscuit in their diet; it is the biscuit which helps to form bulk in the stool. Give a more balanced diet, for apart from anything else trouser washing is not a pleasant job for either dog or owner.

Ear trouble

The dog may hold its head on one side, and shake it. If canker is the cause, treatment can be given long before this stage is reached, because canker can be smelt and should normally be noticed when grooming.

The Shih Tzu grows hair in its ears, and if this is not gently removed it must be kept free from matting and clogging up with wax. Provided the ears are examined regularly from puppyhood, the animal seldom objects later, but it is when they are neglected and pain is caused that treatment becomes very difficult.

If the ear is smelling but not discharging, you can put in ear drops of some proprietary product. I use Otodex, and this drains and clears the ear. Do not prod around inside, but gently wipe the inside of the flap. Powders tend to clog up the ear canal, and should not be used unless specifically ordered by your veterinary surgeon. The same applies to peroxide, which may give off gases and cause internal pressure. Do not leave an ear to become worse, but consult the vet in good time. Never probe inside, for you may pierce the ear-drum.

Eyes

The eyes of the Shih Tzu are vulnerable to accident, and need daily care. If an ulcer forms it should be treated as soon as possible; an untreated ulcer can lead to blindness or even the loss of the eye. If your dog goes for rough country walks, it is a wise precaution to allow the hair to fall over the eyes for protection – the dog will be quite able to see through it. Castor oil is a safe and soothing first-aid treatment for a sore eye, but obtain the right ointment as soon as you can. Better still, keep some in your first-aid box; your veterinary surgeon will supply you with a suitable ointment.

To bathe an eye you will need cotton wool, warm water or

saline solution (one teaspoon salt to one pint water) or you can use Optrex. Have the solution at blood heat, then dip the cotton-wool swab into the lotion and squeeze it gently into the eye from the outer corner, flooding the eye. Repeat this several times.

Fungus

Dogs who lie around on damp grass or earth often get little black spots which are a minute fungus. These stick into the skin in places where there is no coat, especially round the nipples of bitches, and cause irritation. To cure, you can either wash with sulphur soap or use a cloth wrung out in a mixture of two parts of alcohol to one of chloroform, which you can have made up by a chemist; two or more applications may be sufficient, with an interval between.

Grass seed

Hardly an ailment, but included because in the summer months it is most important to watch for grass seed, especially barley. This gets into the coat and thence through to the skin where it lodges itself wherever it can – under the armpits, up the ear flaps and between the pads of the feet. If it is not found and removed, abscesses are likely to form and cause a great deal of trouble and pain.

Lameness

This may be due to neglect of the feet. Hair grows in between the pads of the feet, and it is best to cut this away, unless the dog goes for rough country walks when it can give protection from thorns and snake bites. If the dog is always on a grass run, the hair grows long and then becomes twisted up round the nails, forming hard mats between the pads.

Neglected toenails and dew claws can also cause lameness. If these have grown too long, only a small tip should be taken off at a time since the quick also grows and this needs to shrink back after each cutting. With some nails it is better to use a file.

Tar from the roads can be removed from the pads with acetone. Afterwards, smear Vaseline on the pads.

Cracked pads, which may get small stones or grit or dirt in them, need bathing in warm water, followed by the application of a little healing ointment and a sock worn on the foot until the cut is healed.

Scratching

This can be a great problem. If you have a scratching Shih Tzu, it is unlikely to have a good coat, for the front will remain short and the back will grow long. The best thing to do is to eliminate the various causes one by one, and you might hit on the right one!

Check the anal glands, and for internal and external parasites. Combings from the coat will show the presence of fleas if none are to be seen otherwise. Some dogs are allergic to just one flea bite.

If you live near sheep, make sure the dog has not picked up a sheep tick. Do *not* pull it out, but apply methylated spirit which will cause it to drop off. The tick's head becomes buried under the skin, and an abscess may be caused if the head is left behind.

Harvest mites can also cause a great deal of irritation; these are extremely small, and may be seen around the stomach area, shining like red grains of sand if the sun or bright light is on them. If you know there are harvest mites in your vicinity, dip the dog's feet in permanganate of potash before going for a walk.

Incorrect diet is a frequent cause of scratching. In summer a long-coated dog can easily become overheated, when it may be wise to cut down on his meat intake and give one teaspoon of milk of magnesia. There may be insufficient fat in the diet – this can give rise to scurf which in itself can cause irritation and scratching. One teaspoon of corn oil added to the food, plus a bath with Selsun, will remove scurf.

According to E. P. Stalling – a Houston veterinarian – as recorded in *Dog World*, there is a condition in dogs whereby the passage of food through the digestive system is prolonged owing to the ingestion of dust, swallowing of hair, various bacteria and indigestible materials. This prolonged process sets up a toxic condition, and an alkaline pH of the skin is produced which is normally slightly acid. This leads to a drop in the resistance of the skin to the invasion of bacteria and fungi, and a susceptibility to allergens. To control this situation, it is suggested that one teaspoon of mineral oil to each 7–8 lb of body weight should be given bi-weekly. This should be administered on an empty stomach, in the morning, no food or water being given until the afternoon of the same day. However, this treatment will not cure 'flea allergy dermatitis' if this is already established, and a thorough cleansing of the digestive system is necessary. I have known Shih Tzu owners to be in despair over scratching, when no amount of medicated baths and veterinary treatment seemed able to cure the animal.

Irritation of the skin can also be caused by insufficient grooming. Matting of the coat means that no air can get to the skin, so it is essential to use your comb. Scurf also collects under the mats and causes further irritation.

If the dog is scratching because of any skin lesion, your vet should be consulted for expert advice. It may be necessary to take skin scrapings. Through scratching, a simple irritation and breaking of the skin can very easily lead to a bacterial infection, therefore persistent scratching should never be neglected.

Snorting

I have called this rather distressing condition by this simple name because I cannot think of another sufficiently good one. The complaint is well known to many Shih Tzu owners; the dog appears to both snort and choke, makes a terrible noise and cannot get his breath. He must if possible be made to swallow, either by putting your finger over his nose which will force him to breathe through his mouth, or by putting your finger down his throat which will clear any mucous which may be lodged there. The condition seems to be brought on through excitement or emotion.

Stings

Catching wasps is a great game, but this invariably results in a sting on the lip or – more seriously – in the mouth or throat, although my veterinarian assures me the latter seldom happens. However, if it does occur, adrenalin or cortisone injections must be given at once. The area around the mouth, or any other affected part, can be bathed with a concentration of one tablespoon of household

M

bicarbonate of soda in one to two pints of water; this is quite harmless if accidentally swallowed. Ordinary washing soda may be used instead, and a sting left in should be removed; this usually happens in the case of a bee sting, and vinegar or onion should be applied. Bathing should be continued for about ten minutes, and can be repeated every further ten minutes until the irritation has subsided.

Tartar

If this is left to accumulate on the teeth, the dog will lose them prematurely. Chewing dog biscuits will help to keep the teeth clean, and the new toothpaste called 'Showite' is extremely helpful if used regularly as a preventative measure.

Travel sickness

Few dogs who have been acclimatised to car travel when very young suffer from travel sickness. Some of this sickness is due to fear, and the association of fear. Here is a useful quotation taken from the 'Veterinary Diary' in the *Dog World*: 'The motivation of travel sickness in dogs, appears to be different from that in humans, and for that reason human remedies do not help.'

First, try sitting in a stationary vehicle parked outside the house, to show your dog that no harm will come to him. Then, a day or two later, take him for a short trip around the block, gradually increasing the time spent in the car.

Once the initial hurdle has been overcome, extend the time period, but give a small drink of milk and glucose half an hour before the journey and keep him on the floor of the car for a while so that he doesn't notice the moving objects going by as the car starts. The length of these trips should be gradually increased, and conversely the time spent on the floor of the car decreased. Use antiemetic tranquillising pills, which can be obtained from your veterinary surgeon, and should be given about thirty minutes prior to the journey; continue doing this for four to eight weeks, and by this time some satisfactory progress should have been made.

Vomiting

This does not necessarily mean that something is seriously amiss, but any dog who vomits should be watched, and if the sickness is accompanied by diarrhoea it must be treated professionally. A Shih Tzu vomits quite easily, and if there is a collection of gas in the stomach the dog may bring up a frothy liquid. It is not a good thing to fast a Shih Tzu for too long; indeed, many of them, particularly the smaller ones, do better on two meals daily. If a dog is sick, never press food on it for it probably knows best whether or not it wants to eat. Note the type of vomit, and if there is stale and undigested food the dog could be sickening from some infection. Frequently hair is vomited, but this is quite normal, especially in long-haired breeds, and your dog will not appreciate being starved of his meal for this reason!

Hereditary defects

It is most difficult to discover where the defects lie when coming into a new breed. Breeders are reluctant to admit to anything but perfection in their stock, but nothing is perfect and if an animal should be faultless its antecedents are most unlikely to be the same. However, because a line carries a minor defect, it does not mean it should never by used. The bad points must be weighed against the good, but dogs carrying any severe defect should not be used for breeding; of course there are unavoidable circumstances when the defect does not actually show in the make-up of the dog but lies in a hidden recessive gene.

There are beauty defects and structural defects. The first are important from the show angle, but structural defects are of the utmost importance from every angle. These may be due to hereditary diseases, or to breeding for exaggerated show points, which can do just as much to ruin a breed and indeed has done so in many cases. Take as an example the over-large heads; heads should not, of course, be too small, but exaggerated size will bring its own problems as also will too short a leg and too short a nose, none of which features do anything to help the Shih Tzu. Personally, I would class the exaggerated show points as hereditary defects.

Some congenital hereditary diseases in the whelp have been listed in Chapter 10.

As yet, there is no widespread hereditary disease which is peculiar to the Shih Tzu. Though cases of hip dysplasia have been reported, this is not common in the breed. At present there is no 'normal' hip for comparison, and this makes it difficult to accurately prove whether or not there is a minor degree of dysplasia present. The animal requires a general anaesthetic in order for an X-ray to be taken, and to subject unsuspected stock to this as a matter of routine, without a normal specimen for comparison and control does not make sense to me. However, any suspect stock should most certainly be X-rayed, and on no account used for breeding unless cleared.

Sublaxation of the patella. There have been some cases of this; while it is not widespread as in many toy breeds, with the Shih Tzu becoming smaller it is something which needs to be watched.

Teeth anomalies. This is possibly due to a mutation, but is certainly inherited. Some dogs have only three or even two incisors in the top or bottom jaw. According to Aitchinson in 1962, 'anomalies of the teeth are associated in human congenital osteodystrophies with faulty calcification of membranous bones and of the femurs and extremities.' Also, in 1964, in *Dentition of Short Muzzled Dogs*, it was stated that dental anomalies are frequently accompanied by faulty calcification of membranous bones. According to R. H. Smythe, in *The Breeding and Rearing of Dogs*, boxers carrying the seventh incisor have sometimes developed an abnormal calcification of limb bones in which enlargement of the lower end of one radius has developed, frequently being associated with bone cysts, severe lameness and pain. Up to 1969 this condition had not responded to treatment.

I do not know of any Shih Tzu carrying a seventh incisor, except when a deciduous tooth has been retained. Many have only four in each jaw, but I understand that this is common to breeds of the brachycephalic dog.

Tooth peculiarities should not be treated too lightly in view of reports on other short-headed breeds.

Tight nostrils. This condition appears to be inherited, and there are two types: one in which the nostril is so tight that it is deformed, and this can be seen at birth. In the other form, the nostril may be open and wide at birth, then tighten at ten to twenty-one days, whether from infection or varying growth rates seems uncertain but it can be critical for the whelp. There is more about this in Chapter 10. It may also happen around eight weeks, and the pup will not grow out of it until after the second teeth are cut. Sudden changes of temperature make breathing more difficult for these puppies, but as a rule it does not trouble them once they are past the sucking stage.

Heart disease. I hear of more deaths from heart disease than anything else except road casualties. This can, of course, be heart failure due to old age, but heart disease can also affect the younger animal, and there appear to be several instances of this in the Shih Tzu. There are varying forms which are by no means all inherited, and I have heard no reports that it is familial in the breed.

13

The Shih Tzu Overseas

U.S.A.

It was in 1938 that the first Shih Tzu were exported from this country to the U.S.A. They were two bitches, Ding-ling of the Mynd and Wuffy of the Mynd, bred by Mrs. Harold Eaden. Four others followed, which were all re-registered as Apsos, and in fact this continued until the early 1950s since the American Kennel Club did not recognise the breed at that time.

By 1960 three Shih Tzu clubs had been formed in America: the Texas Shih Tzu Society, the Shih Tzu Club of America, and the American Shih Tzu Association along the east coast. The breed was now recognised by the A.K.C. inasmuch as it could be shown in miscellaneous classes, but the fight for a separate register continued.

In early 1963 the three American clubs merged to form the American Shih Tzu Club, and thereafter combined their efforts to maintain a registry and meet the requirements for recognition by the A.K.C. In the first combined Registry Stud Book published in July 1963, 369 Shih Tzu of both American and foreign breeding were recorded. During the period from 1960 until the end of 1963, England exported seventy-seven animals to the States.

On April 1st 1969 the A.K.C. granted the breed registration in their Stud Book. There were then about three thousand animals registered with the American Shih Tzu Club which became eligible for registration in the A.K.C. foundation Stud Book for the breed. During the period from 1960 to the end of 1969 there had been 642 imports from England.

From September 1969 the Shih Tzu were permitted to be shown for championship points at A.K.C. shows in the toy group. It is worth recording that the system of awarding points towards a champion title is very different from our own. Ninety-three champion Shih Tzu were recorded between September 1st 1969 and December 31st 1970, of both American and foreign breeding.

Ch. Sitsang Whiz Bang, bred by Jane Ambroson, won the the Beely Trophy for the top winning Shih Tzu of 1970, and Ch. Witches Wood Soket Tumi, bred by Marilyn M. Guiraud, won the Rawlings perpetual trophy for the top winning Shih Tzu owned by an A.S.T.C. member. Both were American bred. Points for awarding these trophies were estimated by the Phillips system.

Prior to recognition in 1969, when it was permitted to show the breed in miscellaneous classes, the first American-bred Shih Tzu to gain a championship anywhere were Mexican Ch. Mei-Lei's Pao Ting Fu, his litter sister Mei-Lei's Si An Fu of Kathway's, and Mexican Ch. Mei-Lei's Ming So Tsu of Kathway's; these were bred by Dr. E. M. Holms from English and Australian imported stock.

The first speciality show to be recognised by the A.K.C. at which championship points were awarded was sponsored by the A.S.T.C. and held on May 5th 1973 at Portland, Oregon, in conjunction with the Annual General Meeting of the A.S.T.C. This is another step forward in the American history of the breed.

Mr. Phillip Price and his aunt, Miss Maureen Murdock, were among the first to import and breed Shih Tzu in America. He bought Golden Si Wen of Chasmu whilst visiting London in 1954, and subsequently imported Ho Lai Sheum of Yram in 1955.

In 1960 two French champions were brought in, a dog Ch. Pukedals Ding Dang by Yvette Duval (Albright) and a bitch Ch. Jungfältets Jung Wu by Ingrid Colwell. These were both of Scandinavian breeding, and there are no French blood lines in America up to the time of writing. These were followed by imports from Australia, Canada, England and Scandinavian countries.

Some of the early breeders and kennel names appearing in the pedigrees of dogs in America today, many of whom are still breeding and exhibiting Shih Tzu, are as follows:

Bill-Ora	Mr. and Mrs. Will Mooney
Encore	Mrs. Jane Fitts
Harmony	Miss Maureen Murdock
Jaisu	Miss Su Kaufman and Miss Jay Ammon
Jo-Wil	Mr. J. D. Curtice
Judlu	Mr. and Mrs. George Houston

Kwan Yin	Mrs. Brenda Ostencio
La-Mi	Mr. and Mrs. Charles Gardner
Mariljac	Mr. and Mrs. Jack Wood
Mogene	Mr. and Mrs. Gene Dudgeon
Pako	Mrs. Yvette Duval (Albright)
Rosemar	Mrs. Ann Hickok (Warner)
Sangchen	Mrs. Pat Michael
Shu Lin	Mr. and Mrs. S. Bashore
Si Kiang	Mrs. Ingrid Colwell
Silver Nymph	Mrs. Theresa Drimal
Stonyacres	Mrs. Thelma Ruth
Str-Range	Mr. Joe Strange
Tamworth	Col. and Mrs. J. Lett
Taramount	Mr. and Mrs. Wm. Kibler
Zijuh	Col. and Mrs. F. Loob.

A monthly newsletter, the *Shih Tzu News*, is published by Mr. and Mrs. Gene Dudgeon, and a bi-monthly magazine, *Shih Tzu Bulletin*, is published by the American Shih Tzu Club. Both these publications keep the members well informed of Shih Tzu activities and contain many beautiful pictures.

The breed has rapidly become popular in America, yet it is still a young breed to the country. I regret that there is insufficient space to allow mention of some special dogs; moreover, it is too early and hence too difficult for me to assess lines and families – were I to attempt this I should be sure to offend you all! I might be prepared to risk doing so if I were personally certain of my facts, but reports from other people on the merit of individual dogs should not be put into print.

Australia

In 1954 Mr. and Mrs. Dobson brought their kennel of Shih Tzu from England to New South Wales. This consisted of two dogs, black and white Pei Ho of Taishan (litter brother to Ch. Wang Poo of Taishan), Wen Chin of Lhakang, a chestnut and white dog puppy, and one black bitch Chloe of Elfann. These three were not closely related, and carried the full range of colours in their make-up.

From the first litter, which was sired by Pei Ho of Taishan and born in quarantine, the Shih Tzu infiltrated into other Australian states. One bitch went to South Australia, and from the second litter – sired by Wen Chin of Lhakang, another bitch went to Queensland. The breed was introduced into Victoria in 1957 and into Western Australia shortly afterwards.

At the end of 1959 the original stock was owned by Mrs. Avery of New South Wales, one of whose puppies went with the Queensland stock to Victoria as foundation of the Geltree kennel of Mrs. Gwen Teele.

In 1958 a bitch Hia Nan of Snaefell (full sister to Ch. Sindi Lu of Antarctica) was imported from England to the Geltree kennel, to be joined a year later by a dog Ty Yung of Antarctica. Since those early days there have been further imports to various States which have been chosen with care to give fresh blood lines: two bitches to Western Australia; one dog and one bitch to South Australia; one additional dog to Victoria; one dog and one bitch which came ahead of immigrating Mr. and Mrs. J. Thompson and stayed in Victoria for some months before going to Queensland; three dogs and one bitch to New South Wales. Dogs have also been imported to New Zealand, and their blood lines utilised in Australia. All imports to Australia have come from England or New Zealand.

Shih Tzu have in turn been exported from Australia to U.S.A., Guam, Manila, Malaysia, Japan, Germany, Spain and Singapore.

A newsletter was brought out in 1958 which was circulated throughout Australia as a forerunner to a private club started later the same year. In 1964 this Club was granted Kennel Club affiliation, and given permission to hold an 'Open Parade' for non-champions only, and following this an 'Open Championship Show'. These events were held in Victoria, the home state of the Club. There is now a semi-specialist breed show held in New South Wales and sponsored by the Asian Breeds Club.

Each Australian State has its own governing Kennel Club body, which maintains a separate State Register. Since the Australian Kennel Clubs are affiliated to the English Kennel Club, all breeds on the English Register are accepted with full championship status. However, in Australia the method of gaining the title of Champion is different from that here in England. Classes at shows are regulated by the Kennel Club of the governing State, and C.C.s are given value under a points system according

186 THE SHIH TZU

to the number exhibited at each show for each sex in a breed. One hundred points is the number required, the minimum being four C.C.s under four different judges.

Scandinavia

The Shih Tzu was first introduced into Norway in 1932 by Henrik and Mme. Kauffmann of the Danish Legation, who brought with them one dog and two bitches which they had acquired while residing in China. Information regarding these early imports is in Chapter 2, where you can also read about the comparisons made with the English dogs brought in by the Brownriggs. Mrs. Hyerdahl, who possessed a puppy from an early litter and was a close friend of Mme. Kauffmann, came to England in 1935 to confirm the similarity of the breeds, for at that time they were still referred to as Lhasa Terriers in Norway and Mme. Kauffmann was anxious to ensure their correct registration. The Norsk Kennel Club did not at first recognise the name of Shih Tzu for these dogs, but after direct correspondence with the Shih Tzu Club of England and a comparison between the standards of the Lhasa Terrier and the Shih Tzu, they finally did so in October 1939.

In 1935 a bitch Amoy (sire Yangtze of Taishan, dam Tzu Hsi of Taishan) was sent from England to Mr. Walter Ekman in Sweden; he already owned one Shih Tzu dog which he had brought with him from China.

In the early 1940s Miss Astrid Jepperson started her famous Bjorneholms kennel of Shih Tzu in Denmark; she had purchased her foundation bitch, Mai Ling Tzu au Dux, from Mr. Normann of Oslo, and this came from the Kauffmann stock. The Bjorneholms kennel did much to further the breed in Scandinavia.

In 1955 Mrs. Jungefeldt of Sweden introduced the first Shih Tzu, a bitch Bjorneholms Pippi, into her well-known Jungfältets kennel of Airedales. In 1958, following a visit to England, she imported Fu Ling of Clystvale, who became a strong stud influence and sired over twenty-five C.C. winners in Sweden. His name will be on many pedigrees, including those of exports to America. In return Jungfältets Jung Ming was sent to Mrs. Longden of the Clystvale Kennel in England. At this time registrations in Sweden numbered seventy-one, and have since risen rapidly. In Scandinavia the Shi Tzu is judged in the toy group.

The bitch Jungfältets Jung Wu, owned by Mrs. Ingrid Colwell, was taken to America after being made a French champion.

In Finland lines from England have been introduced, including those of Cherholmes and Lochrenza.

Canada

I have no record of the exact date when the breed was first introduced into Canada, but it was already established in 1935.

Mr. and Mrs. Patrick Morgan of the Chouette kennel were early enthusiasts, as was Miss Margaret Torrible (Mrs. Burbank) of the Kokonor kennels. The Shih Tzu went under many names, including that of Tibetan Terrier, and those sold to the U.S.A. were mostly registered under the name of Lhasa Terrier. Discussion subsequently took place between these breeders and the Shih Tzu Club of England, with regard to their dogs being registered as Shih Tzu in Canada.

An import from England went to the Chouette kennel in Canada in 1935, and three came to England from that kennel in 1938. Unfortunately two of the latter died, but Tashi of Chouette survived and went on to strengthen the English lines.

Hooza, of the Chouette kennel, was fawn and came from Peking. Mingk, from the same kennel, was described as pepper and white in colour and came from Czechoslovakia.

The breed was now rapidly increased in popularity in Canada, and is shown in the non-sporting group.

APPENDIX A

Breed Registrations at the Kennel Club

1934	39	1954	71
1935	20	1955	80
1936	31	1956	97
1937	18	1957	110
1938	28	1958	132
1939	47	1959	133
1940	11	1960	153
1941	11	1961	226
1942	7	1962	276
1943	2	1963	355
1944	12	1964	447
1945	3	1965	499
1946	5	1966	498
1947	10	1967	540
1948	28	1968	771
1949	42	1969	1037
1950	40	1970	1526
1951	60	1971	1453
1952	53	1972	1441
1953	41	1973	1583

APPENDIX B

Breed Clubs

THE SHIH TZU CLUB
Secretary, Charles Duke, 7 Middleton Road, Rotherham, Yorks.
   Rotherham, 70595.

THE MANCHU SHIH TZU SOCIETY
Secretary, Mrs. D. Harding, 4 Montgomery Road, Coombe Glen,
   Uphatherly, Cheltenham, Glos. Cheltenham 31240.

Champions 1949–1973

Name	Sex	Birth	Sire	Dam	Breeder	Owner
1949 Ta Chi of Taishan	B	5.6.45	Sui-Yan	Madam Ko of Taishan	Lady Brownrigg	Breeder
Yu Mo Chuang of Boydon	D	1.8.39	Yangtze of Taishan	Hsueh Li Chan of Taishan	Mrs. H. L. Moulton	Lady Brownrigg
1950 Choo-Ling	D	30.5.44	Sanus Ching-a-Boo	Sing-Pu	Gen. Telfer-Smollett	Lady Brownrigg
1951 Sing Tzu of Shebo	B	11.10.47	Ch. Choo-Ling	Sing-Hi	Mrs. G. Garforth-Bles	Mrs. S. Bode
Shebo Tserno of Lhakang	D	29.4.48	Pu of Oulton	Lindi-lu of Lhakang	Mrs. G. Widdrington	Mrs. S. Bode
Mao-Mao of Lhakang	B	13.6.48	Lyemun of Taishan	Nee-Na of Taishan	Mrs. G. Widdrington	Breeder
1952 Hong of Hungjao	D	10.12.46	Pu of Oulton	Sing-Pu	Gen. Telfer-Smollett	Mrs. H. Eaden
Pa-Ko of Taishan	B	6.4.50	Ch. Yu Mo Chuang of Boydon	Ch. Sing Tzu of Shebo	Mrs. S. Bode	Lady Brownrigg
1953 Ling-Fu of Shuanghsi	B	16.2.51	Lyemun of Taishan	Wu-Ling of Shaunghsi	Mrs. J. Hopkinson	Mr. & Mrs. K. B. Rawlings

Name	Sex	Birth	Sire	Dam	Breeder	Owner
Tensing of Lhakang	D	23.7.52	Ch. Yu Mo Chuang of Boydon	Ch. Mao-Mao of Lhakang	Mrs. G. Widdrington	Mr. & Mrs. K. B. Rawlings
1955 Wang-Poo of Taishan	D	29.2.52	Ch. Choo-Ling	Ch. Pa-Ko of Taishan	Lady Brownrigg	Breeder
Maya Wong of Lhakang	B	23.7.52	Ch. Yu Mo Chuang of Boydon	Ch. Mao-Mao of Lhakang	Mrs. G. Widdrington	Breeder
1956 Lily-Wu of Lhakang	B	23.7.52	Ch. Yu Mo Chuang of Boydon	Ch. Mao-Mao of Lhakang	Mrs. G. Widdrington	Mr. & Mrs. K. B. Rawlings
Yi Ting Mo of Antarctica	D	11.3.53	Ch. Shebo Tsemo of Lhakang	Tang of Oulton	Mr. & Mrs. K. B. Rawlings	Breeders
1957 Shu-Ssa of Michelcombe	B	11.5.54	Ch. Shebo Tsemo of Lhakang	Chuanne Tu of Elfann	Miss O. I. Nichols	Mrs. R. A. Clarke
Yano Okima of Antarctica	D	28.3.55	Perky Ching of the Mynd	Ch. Sing Tzu of Shebo	Mr. & Mrs. K. B. Rawlings	Breeders
1958 Elfann Ta-To of Lhakang	B	13.2.52	Yenmo of Lhakang	Chenmo of Lhakang	Mrs. Mather	Mrs. Murray-Kerr
Shu-She Yu of Lhakang	B	23.7.52	Ch. Yu Mo Chuang of Boydon	Ch. Mao-Mao of Lhakang	Mrs. G. Widdrington	Mrs. Haycock
Sindi-Lu of Antarctica	B	2.10.56	Ch. Yi Ting Mo of Antarctica	Chao-Meng Fu of Antarctica	Mrs. A. L. Dadds	Mr. & Mrs. K. B. Rawlings

1959 Choo-Choo of Cathay	D	30.5.57	Wen Shu of Lhakang	Ta-Le Shih of Tawnyridge	Mrs. J. Ross	Mrs. A. O. Grindey
1960 Tien Memsahib	B	16.6.56	Bimbo	Mu Ho	Mrs. T. E. Morgan	Mrs. G. Widdrington
Suki of Mavesyn	B	28.5.57	Ch. Yi Ting Mo of Antarctica	Yet Ming of Mavesyn	Mrs. M. Cope	Mr. & Mrs. K. B. Rawlings
Shebo Wen Yin of Lhakang	D	7.6.57	Wen Shu of Lhakang	Ch. Maya Wong of Lhakang	Mrs. G. Widdrington	Mrs. S. Bode
Tzu-An of Lhakang	B	12.6.58	Jo-Jo of Lhakang	Mei-Hua of Lhakang	Mrs. F. M. Bunk	Mrs. A. O. Grindey
1961 Jou-Li of Lhakang	B	11.5.55	Bimbo	Ch. Maya Wong of Lhakang	Mrs. G. Widdrington	Mr. P. Beeley
Kuan Ti of Antarctica	D	27.2.57	Ch. Yi Ting Mo of Antarctica	Ch. Ling-Fu of Shuanghsi	Mr. & Mrs. K. B. Rawlings	Breeders
Clystvale Kari of Snowland	D	27.8.59	Khan Janmayen	Tzu-Hsi of Clystvale	Mrs. A. L. Westcott	Miss E. Clark
1962 Pan-Wao Chen of Antarctica	D	18.5.60	Ch. Yi Ting Mo of Antarctica	Dang Gau of Shanghoo	Mrs. St. John Gore	Mr. & Mrs. K. B. Rawlings
Ellingham Kala Nag	D	20.7.59	Tackla Sahib of Lhakang	Darzee of Clystvale	Lady Haggerston	Mrs. J. Lovely
1963 Li Ching Ku of Snaefell	D	4.2.60	Yibbin of Antarctica	Missee-Lee of Snaefell	Mrs. A. L. Dadds	Breeder

Name	Sex	Birth	Sire	Dam	Breeder	Owner
Sumi San of Darli	B	28.2.59	Lundhouse Ping	Coral of Airlea	Miss S. E. Gill	Mr. & Mrs. S. W. Jobson
Su Si of Snaefell	B	28.10.59	Tzu-Hang of Snaefell	Chung of Snaefell	Mrs. A. L. Dadds	Breeder
Teresa of Tinkertown	B	13.1.62	Ch. Kuan Ti of Antarctica	Ah Mei of Lhakang	Mr. P. Beeley	Mrs. Balmforth
1964						
Shiraz of Ellingham	B	17.5.60	Tackla Sahib of Lhakang	Michelcombe Chrystal of Clystvale	Lady Haggerston	Miss E. Evans
Soong of Lhakang	B	1.11.61	Chuangtse of Lhakang	Ching-Yo of Elfann	Mrs. G. Widdrington	Breeder
Talifu Fu Hi	D	11.1.62	Lhakang Li-Shan of Elfann	Lotus Bud of Ricksoo	Mr. & Mrs. C. C. Boot	Breeders
Mei-Saki of Greenmoss	B	5.1.63	Yu Li Ching of Wyndtoi	Sasha Ming of Wyndtoi	Mr. & Mrs. A. Leadbitter	Mrs. Roberts
Shang Wu of Antarctica	B	12.4.63	Ch. Pan Wao Chen of Antarctica	Chia of Antarctica	Mr. & Mrs. K. B. Rawlings	Mr. J. Moody
1965						
Susie Wong of Antarctica	B	10.11.59	Shebo Wenyin of Lhakang	Ch. Su-Ki of Mavesyn	Mr. & Mrs. K. B. Rawlings	Breeders
Chi Ma Che of Antarctica	D	23.5.61	Jungfältets Jung Ming	Elfann Tara of Clystvale	Mrs. Longden	Mr. & Mrs. K. B. Rawlings
Cathay Nicholas of Kashmoor	D	15.8.62	Panpipes Fen Ya	Kandy of Kashmoor	Mrs. N. Ross	Mrs. A. O. Grindey

Name	Sex	Date	Sire	Dam	Owner	Breeders
Tensing of Shanreta	D	17.11.62	Tensing Tu of Telota	Nectarine of Lochnager	Mr. & Mrs. J. R. Smith	Breeders
Talifu Bossy Boots	D	23.1.63	Ch. Talifu Fu-Hi	Lotus Bud of Ricksoo	Mr. & Mrs. C. C. Boot	Breeders
Domese of Telota	B	26.10.63	Ch. Tensing of Shanreta	Siew-Sing of Pagodaland	Mrs. Preedy	Mrs. O. Newson
Greenmoss Chin-Ki of Meo	D	19.1.62	Choo T'Sun of Telota	Elfann Maya Wen of Ricksoo	Mrs. Reynolds	Mr. & Mrs. Leadbitter
1967 Dott of Gorseycop	B	1.9.63	Snaefell Huckleberry Finn	Sukie Tong of Dapperlee	Mrs. M. Bennett	Mrs. M. Hoare
Quan-Shu of Edsville	D	27.12.63	Greenmoss Yu-Li-Ching of Wyndtoi	Shang Tsi of Manjuariu	Mr. E. Openshaw	Breeder
Ling-Fu of Antarctica	B	17.5.64	Longlane Telstar	Domus Yanda	Miss E. L. Bennett	Mr. & Mrs. Rawlings
Susella of Banwee	B	22.7.65	Sy-Chim of Banwee	Ming-Lu of Shanreta	Mesdames Tomlinson & Godson	Mrs. T. E. Morgan
Antarctica Chan Shih of Darite	D	7.8.65	Ch. Chi-Ma-Che of Antarctica	Fu-Chi of Darite	Mrs. Copplestone	Mr. & Mrs. K. B. Rawlings
Katrina of Greenmoss	B	9.9.65	Ch. Greenmoss Chin-Ki of Meo	Mei Lu-Lu of Wyndtoi	Mr. & Mrs. A. Leadbitter	Breeders
Golden Peregrine of Elfann	D	20.2.66	Sing-Hi of Lhakang	Golden Bobbin of Elfann	Miss E. Evans	Mr. & Mrs. A. Leadbitter
1968 Kuang-Kuang of Antarctica	D	3.9.62	Ch. Chi-Ma-Che of Antarctica	Sing-Tzu of Antarctica	Mr. & Mrs. K. B. Rawlings	Breeders

Name	Sex	Birth	Sire	Dam	Breeder	Owner
Ah Hsuen Li-Chan of Cathay	D	14.4.64	Ch. Cathay Nicholas Kashmoor	Kin-Po Clystvale	Mrs. A. O. Grindey	Breeder
Fleeting Yu-Sing of Antarctica	D	19.8.65	Ch. Pan Wao Chen of Antarctica	Fleeting Banwee Ming	Mrs. M. Garrish	Mr. & Mrs. K. B. Rawlings
Lochranza Choo-Ling of Cathay	B	16.5.66	Ch. Cathay Nicholas of Kashmoor	Lochranza Lolita of Barusann	Misses MacMillan & Coull	Mrs. A. O. Grindey
1969 Yu Chin Wong	B	1.4.65	Tensing Tu of Telota	Tiger Lily of Myarlune	Mr. C. Howe	Breeder
Cherholme Singing Lady of Wysarge	B	4.5.66	Greenmoss Yu-Li-Ching of Wyndtoi	Cherholme Buckdene Kin Ying Hwa	Mrs. Reithermann	Mrs. M. Coppage
1970 Jen Kai Ko of Lhakang	D	3.3.67	Sing Hi of Lhakang	Jessame of Lhakang	Mrs. G. Widdrington	Mrs. E. J. Fox
Chesaki of Antarctica	B	16.4.68	Ch. Antarctica Chan Shih of Darite	Gina of Antarctica	Mr. & Mrs. K. B. Rawlings	Breeders
Greenmoss Golden Sunbeam of Elfann	B	26.4.68	Ch. Golden Peregrine of Elfann	Elfann Sunshine of Greenmoss	Miss E. Evans	Mr. & Mrs. A. Leadbitter
Dominic of Telota	D	2.7.68	Ch. Antarctica Chan Shih of Darite	Ch. Domese of Telota	Mrs. O. Newson	Breeder
Sue-Ling of Bridgend	B	8.12.68	Ch. Greenmoss Chin-Ki of Meo	Tricina Kylin	Mr. & Mrs. E. Carter	Breeders
Ya-Tung of Antarctica	D	1.5.69	Ch. Fleeting Yu Sing of Antarctica	Susannah of Antarctica	Mr. & Mrs. K. B. Rawlings	Breeders

1971						
Che Ko of Antarctica	B	10.4.67	Ch. Antarctica Chan-Shih of Darite	Ch. Shang-Wo of Antarctica	Mr. & Mrs. K. B. Rawlings	Breeders
Chin-Ling of Greenmoss	B	1.9.68	Ch. Greenmoss Chin-Ki of Meo	Hsiang Chieh of Liddesdale	Mrs. J. Mangles	Mr. & Mrs. A. Leadbitter
Tricina Wen Mo of Bridgend	B	8.12.68	Ch. Greenmoss Chin-Ki of Meo	Tricina Kylin	Mr. & Mrs. E. Carter	Breeders
Fei Ying of Greenmoss	B	25.1.69	Ch. Golden Peregrine o Elfann	Brownhills Yu Honey	Mr. & Mrs. A. Leadbitter	Breeders
Antarctica Don Juan of Telota	D	16.2.69	Ch. Fleeting Yu Sing of Antarctica	Ch. Domese of Telota	Mrs. O. Newson	Mr. & Mrs. K. B. Rawlings
Ko-Ko Saki of Greenmoss	B	6.7.69	Ch. Jen Kai Ko of Lhakang	Ch. Mei Saki of Greenmoss	Mr. & Mrs. A. Leadbitter	Breeders
1972						
Kuire Hermes of Antarctica	D	24.2.71	Ch. Ya Tung of Antarctica	Duchess of Telota	Mrs. R. D. Johnson	Mr. & Mrs. K. B. Rawlings
Newroots Nankipoo of Snaefell	D	4.12.70	Ch. Greenmoss Chin-ki of Meo	Ho-yan of Newroots	Misses Fenner & Thomas	Mrs. A. Dadds
Zeus of Bridgend	D	8.12.68	Ch. Greenmoss Chin-ki of Meo	Tricina Kylin	Mr. & Mrs. E. Carter	Mrs. Thornton
Cherholme Golden Samantha	B	20.3.68	Int. Ch. Golden Peregrine of Elfann	Int. Ch. Cherholmes Debutante	Mrs. Reithermann	Breeder
Whitethroats Chinese Gem	B	11.6.70	Ch. Jen Kai Ko of Lhakang	Whitethroats Mei-Ling	Mr. & Mrs. Fox	Breeders

Name	Sex	Birth	Sire	Dam	Breeder	Owner
Mu T'ang of Antarctica	B	2.5.70	Choo Yau Fong of Antarctica	Chan Sophie of Akaben	Mr. & Mrs. K. B. Rawlings	Breeders
Bowstones Shapur of Cathay	D	21.6.69	Ch. Nicholas of Kashmoor	Bowstones Ko Ko Dhu	Mrs. I Booth	Mrs. A. O. Grindey
1973 Greenmoss Soket Tumi	D	19.2.71	Ch. Greenmoss Chin-Ki of Meo	Ch. Greenmoss Golden Sunbeam of Elfann	Mr. & Mrs. A. Leadbitter	Breeders
Sarawana Chiu Mei of Taonan	B	23.8.68	Ch. Greenmoss Chin-Ki of Meo	Sarawana Buckdene Mitsuko	Mr. I. & Miss Wigglesworth	Mrs. D. B. Harding
Kushu Palhi of Shasheen	B	24.11.70	Ch. Ching-Ling of Greenmoss	Shawala Kula	Miss D. M. Bridge	Mrs. M. Turnbull
Keytor Sweet Charity	B	17.11.71	Ch. Greenmoss Chin-ki of Meo	Keytor Sukee Sue of Hyning	Mrs. E. M. Johnson	Breeder
Simone of Sandown	B	19.4.70	Buda Buda of Rawstock	San Yen of Sandown	Mr. W. E. Donaldson	Mr. B. H. Halton
Wysarge Chinki Tuo of Greenmoss	D	20.6.69	Ch. Greenmoss Chin-ki of Meo	Franwil Kiki Dee	Mr. & Mrs. A. Leadbitter	Mrs. E. M. Johnson
Antarctica Ta T'ung Fu	B	15.10.70	Ch. Ya Tung of Antarctica	Chih Shih of Antarctica	Miss K. Willeby	Mr. & Mrs. K. B. Rawlings
Santosha Rambling Rose	B	6.7.70	Ch. Chin Ling of Greenmoss	Marnie of Myatlune	Mr. & Mrs. D. Crossley	Mr. & Mrs. V. Wilkinson

APPENDIX D

AMERICAN STANDARD FOR SHIH TZU

(Reproduced by kind permission of the American Kennel Club)

The Board of Directors of The American Kennel Club has approved the following Standard for Shih Tzu, to be effective September 1, 1969.

GENERAL APPEARANCE: Very active, lively and alert, with a distinctly arrogant carriage. The Shih Tzu is proud of bearing as befits his noble ancestry, and walks with head well up and tail carried gaily over the back.

HEAD: Broad and round, wide between the eyes. Muzzle square and short, but not wrinkled, about one inch from tip of nose to stop. *Definite Stop. Eyes:* Large, dark and round but not prominent, placed well apart. Eyes should show warm expression. *Ears:* Large, with long leathers, and carried drooping; set slightly below the crown of the skull; so heavily coated that they appear to blend with the hair of the neck. *Teeth:* Level or slightly undershot bite.

FOREQUARTERS: Legs short, straight, well boned, muscular, and heavily coated. Legs and feet look massive on account of the wealth of hair.

BODY: Body between the withers and the root of the tail is somewhat longer than the height at the withers; well coupled and sturdy. Chest broad and deep, shoulders firm, back level.

HINDQUARTERS: Legs short, well boned and muscular, are straight when viewed from the rear. Thighs well rounded and muscular. Legs look massive on account of wealth of hair.

FEET: Of good size, firm, well padded, with hair between the pads. Dewclaws, if any, on the hind legs are generally removed. Dewclaws on the forelegs may be removed.

TAIL: Heavily plumed and curved well over the back; carried gaily, set on high.

COAT: A luxurious, long, dense coat. May be slightly wavy but *not* curly. Good woolly undercoat. The hair on top of the head may be tied up.

COLOR: All colors permissible. Nose and eye rims black, except that dogs, with liver markings may have liver noses and slightly lighter eyes.

GAIT: Slightly rolling, smooth and flowing, with strong rear action.

SIZE: Height at withers—9 to 10½ inches—should be no more than 11 inches nor less than 8 inches. Weight of mature dogs—12 to 15 pounds—should be no more than 18 pounds nor less than 9 pounds. However, type and breed characteristics are of the greatest importance.

FAULTS: Narrow head, overshot bite, snipiness, pink on nose or eye rims, small or light eyes, legginess, sparse coat, lack of definite stop.

BIBLIOGRAPHY

Bergman, Göran, *Why Does Your Dog Do That?*, Popular Dogs, 1970.

Burns, Marcia and Fraser, Margaret N., *Genetics of the Dog*, Agricultural Bureau, 1952; Oliver and Boyd, 1966.

Collier, V. W. F., *Dogs of China and Japan in Nature and Art*, Heinemann, 1921.

Easton, Rev. D. Allan and Brearley, Joan McDonald, *This is the Shih Tzu*, T.F.H. Publications, N.D.

Edgson, F. Andrew, M.R.C.V.S., and Gwynne-Jones, Olwen, *First-Aid and Nursing for Your Dog*, Popular Dogs, 1954; 5th edn. 1973.

Frankling, Eleanor, *The Dog Breeder's Introduction to Genetics*, Popular Dogs, 1966.

Frankling, Eleanor, *Practical Dog Breeding and Genetics*, Popular Dogs, 1961; 4th edn. 1974.

Graham, Captain R. Portman, *The Mating and Whelping of Dogs*, Popular Dogs, 1954; 8th edn. 1973.

Gwynne-Jones, Olwen, *The Popular Guide to Puppy-Rearing*, Popular Dogs, 1951; 9th edn. 1973.

Hammond, J., *Growth and The Development of Mutton: Qualities in Sheep*, Oliver and Boyd, 1932.

Lauffer, Berthold, *Chinese Pottery of The Han Dynasty*, E. J. Brill, Leiden, 1909; Charles E. Tuttle, Japan, 1962.

Lu Zee Yuen Nee, Madame, *The Lhassa Lion Dog*, Pekin Kennel Club (International), N.D.; reprinted by Maples Press, Rugby, England. N.D.

Lyon, McDowell, *The Dog in Action*, Howell Book House, 1950 and 1971.

McCay, Clive M., *Nutrition of the Dog*, Comstock, Ithaca, New York, 1943 and 1949.

Pfaffenberger, Clarence, *The New Knowledge of Dog Behavior*, Howel Book House, 1963 and 1971.

Scott, John Paul, and Fuller, John L., *Genetics and Social Behavior of the Dog*, University of Chicago Press, 1965 and 1971.

Smythe, R. H., M.R.C.V.S., *The Breeding and Rearing of Dogs*, Popular Dogs, 1969; 2nd edn. 1972.

Smythe, R. H., M.R.C.V.S., *The Anatomy of Dog Breeding*, Popular Dogs, 1962.

BIBLIOGRAPHY

Snellgrove and Richardson, *A Cultural History of Tibet*, Weidenfeld and Nicolson, 1968.

Widdrington, Gay, *The Shih Tzu Handbook*, 1971.

American Shih Tzu Club Brochure, 1969.

American Shih Tzu Club Bulletin, 1972 (July).

American Shih Tzu Club Stud Book, 1963 (July).

Dudgeon, Gene and Mollie, *Shih Tzu News*, Dudgeon, U.S.A. *Passim.*

Manchu Shih Tzu Society, Newsletter, May/June 1968.

Shih Tzu Club, *Shih Tzu News*, England. *Passim.*

Aitchinson, James, 'Incisor Dentitions of Short-muzzled Dogs', *Veterinary Record*, 1964, Volume 76.

Stokard, Charles, 'Inheritance of Localised Dwarfism and Achondroplasia in Dogs', *American Journal of Anatomy*, 38, 39.

BIBLIOGRAPHY

ALL OWNERS of pure-bred dogs will benefit themselves and their dogs by enriching their knowledge of breeds and of canine care, training, breeding, psychology and other important aspects of dog management. The following list of books covers further reading recommended by judges, veterinarians, breeders, trainers and other authorities. Books may be obtained at the finer book stores and pet shops, or through Howell Book House Inc., publishers, New York.

Breed Books

AFGHAN HOUND, Complete	Miller & Gilbert
AIREDALE, New Complete	Edwards
ALASKAN MALAMUTE, Complete	Riddle & Seeley
BASSET HOUND, Complete	Braun
BEAGLE, Complete	Noted Authorities
BLOODHOUND, Complete	Brey & Reed
BORZOI, Complete	Groshans
BOXER, Complete	Denlinger
BRITTANY SPANIEL, Complete	Riddle
BULLDOG, New Complete	Hanes
BULL TERRIER, New Complete	Eberhard
CAIRN TERRIER, Complete	Marvin
CHESAPEAKE BAY RETRIEVER, Complete	Cherry
CHIHUAHUA, Complete	Noted Authorities
COCKER SPANIEL, New	Kraeuchi
COLLIE, Complete	Official Publication of the Collie Club of America
DACHSHUND, The New	Meistrell
DALMATIAN, The	Treen
DOBERMAN PINSCHER, New	Walker
ENGLISH SETTER, New Complete	Tuck, Howell & Graef
ENGLISH SPRINGER SPANIEL, New	Goodall & Gasow
FOX TERRIER, New Complete	Silvernail
GERMAN SHEPHERD DOG, Complete	Bennett
GERMAN SHORTHAIRED POINTER, New	Maxwell
GOLDEN RETRIEVER, Complete	Fischer
GREAT DANE, New Complete	Noted Authorities
GREAT DANE, The—Dogdom's Apollo	Draper
GREAT PYRENEES, Complete	Strang & Giffin
IRISH SETTER, New	Thompson
IRISH WOLFHOUND, Complete	Starbuck
KEESHOND, Complete	Peterson
LABRADOR RETRIEVER, Complete	Warwick
LHASA APSO, Complete	Herbel
MINIATURE SCHNAUZER, Complete	Eskrigge
NEWFOUNDLAND, New Complete	Chern
NORWEGIAN ELKHOUND, New Complete	Wallo
OLD ENGLISH SHEEPDOG, Complete	Mandeville
PEKINGESE, Quigley Book of	Quigley
PEMBROKE WELSH CORGI, Complete	Sargent & Harper
POMERANIAN, New Complete	Ricketts
POODLE, New Complete	Hopkins & Irick
POODLE CLIPPING AND GROOMING BOOK, Complete	Kalstone
PULI, Complete	Owen
SAMOYED, Complete	Ward
SCHIPPERKE, Official Book of	Root, Martin, Kent
SCOTTISH TERRIER, New Complete	Marvin
SHETLAND SHEEPDOG, The New	Riddle
SHIH TZU, The (English)	Dadds
SIBERIAN HUSKY, Complete	Demidoff
TERRIERS, The Book of All	Marvin
WEST HIGHLAND WHITE TERRIER, Complete	Marvin
WHIPPET, Complete	Pegram
YORKSHIRE TERRIER, Complete	Gordon & Bennett

Breeding

ART OF BREEDING BETTER DOGS, New	Onstott
BREEDING YOUR SHOW DOG, Joy of	Seranne
HOW TO BREED DOGS	Whitney
HOW PUPPIES ARE BORN	Prine
INHERITANCE OF COAT COLOR IN DOGS	Little

Care and Training

DOG OBEDIENCE, Complete Book of	Saunders
NOVICE, OPEN AND UTILITY COURSES	Saunders
DOG CARE AND TRAINING FOR BOYS AND GIRLS	Saunders
DOG NUTRITION, Collins Guide to	Collins
DOG TRAINING FOR KIDS	Benjamin
DOG TRAINING, Koehler Method of	Koehler
GO FIND! Training Your Dog to Track	Davis
GUARD DOG TRAINING, Koehler Method of	Koehler
OPEN OBEDIENCE FOR RING, HOME AND FIELD, Koehler Method of	Koehler
SPANIELS FOR SPORT (English)	Radcliffe
STONE GUIDE TO DOG GROOMING FOR ALL BREEDS	Stone
SUCCESSFUL DOG TRAINING, The Pearsall Guide to	Pearsall
TOY DOGS, Kalstone Guide to Grooming All	Kalstone
TRAINING THE RETRIEVER	Kersley
TRAINING YOUR DOG TO WIN OBEDIENCE TITLES,	Morsell
TRAIN YOUR OWN GUN DOG, How to	Goodall
UTILITY DOG TRAINING, Koehler Method of	Koehler
VETERINARY HANDBOOK, Dog Owner's Home	Carlson & Giffin

General

COMPLETE DOG BOOK, The	Official Publication of American Kennel Club
DISNEY ANIMALS, World of	Koehler
DOG IN ACTION, The	Lyon
DOG BEHAVIOR, New Knowledge of	Pfaffenberger
DOG JUDGE'S HANDBOOK	Tietjen
DOG JUDGING, Nicholas Guide to	Nicholas
DOG PEOPLE ARE CRAZY	Riddle
DOG PSYCHOLOGY	Whitney
DOG STANDARDS ILLUSTRATED	
DOGSTEPS, Illustrated Gait at a Glance	Elliott
ENCYCLOPEDIA OF DOGS, International	Dangerfield, Howell & Riddle
JUNIOR SHOWMANSHIP HANDBOOK	Brown & Mason
MY TIMES WITH DOGS	Fletcher
OUR PUPPY'S BABY BOOK (blue or pink)	
RICHES TO BITCHES	Shattuck
SUCCESSFUL DOG SHOWING, Forsyth Guide to	Forsyth
TRIM, GROOM AND SHOW YOUR DOG, How to	Saunders
WHY DOES YOUR DOG DO THAT?	Bergman
WILD DOGS in Life and Legend	Riddle
WORLD OF SLED DOGS, From Siberia to Sport Racing	Coppinger

INDEX